MUTUAL IMPACT

MUTUAL IMPACT
At the Crossroads
of Psychoanalysis and Literature

Joachim Küchenhoff

PHOENIX
PUBLISHING HOUSE
firing the mind

First published in 2023 by
Phoenix Publishing House Ltd
62 Bucknell Road
Bicester
Oxfordshire OX26 2DS

British Library Cataloguing in Publication Data

A C.I.P. for this book is available from the British Library

ISBN-13: 978-1-800131-682

Typeset by Medlar Publishing Solutions Pvt Ltd, India

www.firingthemind.com

Contents

Acknowledgements

Chapters 1 to 8 were originally published in German. The author would like to thank the publishers of the following articles for their permission to reprint these English-language translations.

Chapter 1. Küchenhoff, J. (2018b). Negativität und Sprache in "King Lear". *Freiburger literaturpsychologische Gespräche. Jahrbuch für Literatur und Psychoanalyse, 37*: 105–127.

Chapter 2. Küchenhoff, J. (2005). Negativität als Bewahrung? Zur individuellen und kulturellen Repräsentation des Nicht-Repräsentierbaren—am Beispiel von H. Melvilles "Bartleby the Scrivener". *Freiburger literaturpsychologische Gespräche. Jahrbuch für Literatur und Psychoanalyse, 24*: 279–298.

Chapter 3. Küchenhoff, J. (2000). Ästhetische Form und unbewusster Sinn—Selbstfürsorge und Identität in "Moby-Dick". *Psyche—Zeitschrift für Psychoanalyse und ihre Anwendungen, 54*: 51–73.

Chapter 4. Küchenhoff, J. (2004). Die Zeit und der Andere im psychoanalytischen Erinnerungsprozess. *Freiburger literaturpsychologische Gespräche. Jahrbuch für Literatur und Psychoanalyse, 23*: 55–66.

Chapter 5. Küchenhoff, J. (2015). Interkulturelle Gewalt und interkulturelle Übergangsräume. Konstruktion und Dekonstruktion des

Fremden. *Freiburger literaturpsychologische Gespräche. Jahrbuch für Literatur und Psychoanalyse, 34*: 21–40.

Chapter 6. Küchenhoff, J. (2017). Jedermann. Das Sterben in Literatur und Psychoanalyse. *Freiburger literaturpsychologische Gespräche. Jahrbuch für Literatur und Psychoanalyse, 36*: 51–67.

Chapter 7. Küchenhoff, J. (2013). Der Körper, der Mangel, die Scham. Freiburger literaturpsychologische Gespräche. *Jahrbuch für Literatur und Psychoanalyse, 32*: 77–91.

Chapter 8. Küchenhoff, J. (2019). Beziehung und Beziehungsarbeit. *Psychosozial, 13*(42): 39–50. https://doi.org/10.30820/0171-3434-2019-1-39

About the author

Joachim Küchenhoff, MD, is a psychoanalyst and member of the International Psychoanalytic Association and of the Swiss and German psychoanalytic societies. He is a specialist in psychiatry/psychotherapy and in psychosomatic medicine, professor emeritus at Basel University, and visiting professor at the International Psychoanalytic University Berlin. He worked as the medical director of the department of adult psychiatry in the canton Baselland, Switzerland, from 2007 to 2018. He was editor-in-chief of the Swiss Archives of Neurology, Psychiatry and Psychotherapy from 2008 to 2021 and is chair of the supervisory board at the IPU Berlin.

He has written seventeen academic books, and in addition has edited twenty-four academic volumes. He has published widely, especially on psychoanalytic topics. The full list of his publications can be found via his homepage (www.praxis-kuechenhoff.ch). He is especially interested in psychoanalytic transdisciplinary research, and so has collaborated intensively with philosophical, cultural, and literary scholars. His scientific work centres on the psychoanalytic approach to severe psychic disorders in psychiatry and psychosomatic medicine and on the subjective body experience (body image).

Introduction

A comprehensive review of the history of psychoanalytic literary criticism

From its outset, psychoanalysis has been concerned with literature. On the one hand, novels, plays, or even lyrics laid the groundwork for and engendered psychoanalytic concepts. The best example is *Oedipus Rex*, written by the Greek dramatist Sophocles in the fifth century BC; Sigmund Freud referred to Sophocles (or the translation presented by the author Hugo von Hofmannsthal) when he coined the term "Oedipus complex" as the central conflict in the neurotic personality, as we all know. On the other hand, from the very beginning, works of literature have been the object of psychoanalytic scrutiny. Freud interpreted various works of literature and art. He summarised in his text *An Autobiographical Study*:

> It was tempting to go on from there to an attempt at an analysis of poetic and artistic creation in general. The realm of imagination was seen to be a "reservation" made during the painful transition from the pleasure principle to the reality principle in

order to provide a substitute for instinctual satisfactions which had to be given up in real life. The artist, like the neurotic, had withdrawn from an unsatisfying reality into this world of imagination; but, unlike the neurotic, he knew how to find a way back from it and once more to get a firm foothold in reality. His creations, works of art, were the imaginary satisfactions of unconscious wishes, just as dreams are; and like them they were in the nature of compromises, since they too were forced to avoid any open conflict with the forces of repression. But they differed from the asocial, narcissistic products of dreaming in that they were calculated to arouse sympathetic interest in other people and were able to evoke and to satisfy the same unconscious wishful impulses in them too. Besides this, they made use of the perceptual pleasure of formal beauty as what I have called an "incentive bonus". What psycho-analysis was able to do was to take the interrelations between the impressions of the artist's life, his chance experiences, and his works, and from them to construct his [mental] constitution and the instinctual impulses at work in it—that is to say, that part of him which he shared with all men.

(1925d, p. 64)

Here, Freud refers to the object of psychoanalytic interpretation of literature: to link the artist's productions to his personal life, and in addition to find out the general mechanisms at work in the psyche.

In 1912, the journal *Imago. Zeitschrift für die Anwendung der Psychoanalyse auf die Geisteswissenschaften* (*Imago: Journal for the Application of Psychoanalysis on Humanities*) was founded by Otto Rank and Hanns Sachs. Ernest Jones wrote an early review one year later. He points out that the new journal

is concerned with the application of psychoanalytic researches and conclusions to the various mental sciences, particularly to pedagogy, religious psychology, mythology, folk-lore, criminology, jurisprudence, theory of morality, aesthetics, philology, and the genesis of art and literature.

(Jones, 1913, p. 66)

From its outset, the journal offered interpretations of literature, for example, Leo Kaplan on "The psychology of tragedy" (1912), Isidor Sadger on "From pathography to psychography" (1912), Hanns Sachs on "Motive formation by Schnitzler" (1913), and Otto Rank on the "Double" (1914).

So, from very early on, psychoanalysis has shown a vivid interest in literature. Let's have a look on the other side: many excellent plays and novels published in the twentieth century owe their content or their form to basic concepts in psychoanalysis. Take James Joyce as an example. Although Joyce adamantly despised psychoanalysis, arguably his main texts *Ulysses* and *Finnegans Wake* would not have been possible without psychoanalytic influences. Samuel Beckett was in psychoanalytic psychotherapy with W. R. Bion, and literary scholars have claimed that a substantial undercurrent of psychoanalytic influences can be detected in Beckett's writings. Soon after Thomas Pynchon's novel *Gravity's Rainbow* was published, its indebtedness to psychoanalytic culture criticism was highlighted. There are countless other examples I could add.

Psychoanalytic literary criticism has changed in focus over the decades. It started off by analysing the author via a psychoanalytically informed reading of the text. This approach was soon questioned using two undeniable counterarguments, the first being that psychoanalysis is reductive, as the text itself is not read on its own merit but serves only as a starting point to derive an interpretation of impulses attributed to the author's unconscious. The other objection was closely linked to this idea of reductivity: whenever complex scenes in, for example, a novel are reduced to well-known psychoanalytic constructs, literary criticism on a psychoanalytic basis tends to evoke boredom, as the same results will always be attained in the end.

Whereas author-related interpretations have been mostly abandoned, a second approach is still in use today. One can see the literary text with a multitude of signs as a reference to the unconscious, indeed it has an unconscious layer itself. It is able to make the absent present—but only indirectly. The text contains unconscious meaning by evoking signs of a different, pre-linguistic kind, such as scenes, interactions, and affects. The signs do not name the unconscious and thereby make it conscious; instead, they are pre-linguistic signs built from consciously perceptible words. Without our consciously perceiving them, they remind us of unconscious structures and provoke unconscious phantasies and emotions, to which they are connected.

Psychoanalysis shifted its main focus of interest from the individual, seen as a single personality, to object relations or a two-persons psychology. As a result, psychoanalysis could much better explore the interpersonal or intersubjective relationship models in clinical contexts. This object relations approach can be applied to literary criticism, widening it to reader-response criticism. In the USA, Norman Holland was especially important for focusing on psychoanalytic criticism. For instance, he developed a model of literary processing based on a psychoanalytic theory of identity, the central argument being that writers create texts as expressions of their personal identities and readers re-create their own identities when they respond to them (e.g. Holland, 1993, 1999).

Last but not least, Jacques Lacan has also had a significant impact on psychoanalytic literary criticism. Lacan posited that the unconscious is structured like a language; he introduced semiotic concepts and theories on symbol formation into psychoanalytic theory. Lacanian theory applied to literary criticism contributed to a major shift in interest. This led to an evaluation and interpretation not only of content but also, and predominantly, of form, for example, of signifiers used in the text—the aesthetics of a given work that make sense or preclude meaning.

Julia Kristeva started by using Lacanian concepts, but soon developed new horizons in text interpretation; she is of the utmost importance for this field because she is a semiotic scholar as well as a practising psychoanalyst. She differentiated the semiotic from the symbolic and made it possible to study, for example, in lyrical works, the infralinguistic affective qualities of the semiotic by using a more "maternal" approach, compared to Lacan's more "paternal" concept of the symbolic. Likewise, her theory of abjection opened up a new scope of interpretation, which allowed for understanding of what is eliminated from the symbolic. Kristeva has explored modern literature such as Dostoyevsky, Proust, or Céline regarding the place of the abject, in order to be able to grasp the breakdown of boundaries, the transgression of subjectivity, and so on (Kristeva, 1984).

Transdisciplinary explorations

Having given a very short overview of concepts in psychoanalytic literary criticism, I will now explain my own approach. I start with a necessary digression.

In all scientific and cultural fields, networking is the essential answer to intra-scientific specialisation. Interdisciplinarity and transdisciplinarity will of necessity be addressed where the individual discipline does not succeed (or no longer succeeds) in grasping the whole of social, cultural, and scientific development. Cultural anthropology and cultural science are currently the most far-reaching umbrella terms for a cross-sectional science based on multidisciplinary foundations and equipped with the expertise of individual disciplines. It has its place within psychoanalysis, claims its place within psychoanalysis, and is needed and used within psychoanalysis. For Freud, it was still self-evident that psychoanalysis had to be not only therapy, but also simultaneously literary analysis, criticism of religion, ethnology, and much more. In the meantime, the field of psychoanalysis, as well as other sciences, has become so differentiated that not one individual, nor one discipline, can maintain an overview. Therefore, today an inter- or transdisciplinary dialogue is essential. In the following section, I prefer and will use only the term "transdisciplinarity", which is understood as a research and scientific principle that becomes effective wherever a merely disciplinary definition of problems and their solutions is no longer possible.

Why this short digression? For me, transdisciplinarity is the base from which to start psychoanalytic literature analysis. It implies a no-priority approach. Psychoanalysis is not above or underlying literature. I know that psychoanalysis has ever so often precluded a true transdisciplinary dialogue, especially by overgeneralising its own findings, by blurring methodological boundaries between psychoanalysis and the cooperating sciences, and—especially in the interpretation of literature and art—by an annoying reductionism. This somewhat arrogant attitude might have been historically justifiable by a "gold-digger" habit motivated by the development of drive theory that used seduction in order to see the gold pieces of drives flashing everywhere. It has widely disappeared; instead, an attitude of modesty has rightly supervened. This enabled psychoanalysts to enter a transdisciplinary dialogue more readily. To face it implies reflecting oneself in the mirror of the other sciences in a distanced and critical manner. Transdisciplinarity thus always involves self-criticism and self-questioning.

Of course, psychoanalysis has much to offer in the transdisciplinary dialogue with literature and literary criticism. I will mention just a few aspects:

1. Unconscious motivations: Psychoanalysis contributes the perspective of unconscious motivations of social action and thought. What escapes the intentions of the conscious subject or the social group becomes observable, nameable, and possibly changeable through psychoanalytic procedures. Psychoanalytic instruments can decipher not only persons, but also cultural encounters.
2. Psyche and interpersonality: Psychoanalysis does not only investigate the intrapsychic on its own, but also includes the interplay of the intrapsychic and the interpersonal, that is, the relationship between individual and social.
3. Interpretive perspectives: Psychoanalysis offers supplementary interpretative strategies and content that are unfamiliar to cultural studies, which in part do not fit into the interpretive patterns of other sciences, and in part are comparable to them. Today, psychoanalysis's position in the context of the humanities can be described differently than it was a few decades ago. Mainly due to Jacques Derrida's deconstructivism, philosophical hermeneutics has modified and extended its concept of understanding. Understanding does not only refer to the (positive) understanding of texts, forms of existence, or conversation, but is also directed at the breaks, the omissions, the voids that are to be deciphered only by means of marginal signs and hints.
4. Microscopic clinical heuristics: Psychoanalysis provides interpretive schemes that stem from clinical contexts and can prove meaningful when applied to cultural phenomena. In this respect, the cumulative in-depth, clinical, individual case experience could function as a microscopic heuristic for the diagnosis of sociocultural developments. For example, in a remarkable contribution to psychoanalytic research on violence, Hermann Beland (1999) rightly made the claim that, as experts of war, psychoanalysts should ask themselves what they have to say about collective wars—and thus also about violence and its end.

5. Critical subject theory: Psychoanalysis is a critical subject theory, which sets out to find expressions of (buried) subjectivity, even where only deficiency and loss might otherwise be visible. Psychoanalytically speaking, the absence of functions can be understood as a form of "negation" or "negation work". This opens up largely unused fields of dialogue with concepts of negativity in philosophy and literary studies.

6. Speech and language: Psychoanalysis examines the dynamics associated with the limitations of utterances and ways of speaking in patients, and it seeks to improve language competence. In doing so, psychoanalysis goes further than the sciences that are concerned only with speech behaviour, because it considers the "existential", the developmental, psychological, and affective preconditions and preliminary stages of speech and thought.

I pointed out that psychoanalysis has much to offer for any transdisciplinary discussion. On the other side, psychoanalytic thinking also profits enormously from literature and literary criticism. The list of aspects psychoanalysis might win from a transdisciplinary dialogue should not be dismissed. Transdisciplinarity is not a one-way dialogue. As I have shown in the first section of this introduction, psychoanalysis has adopted many concepts from literature as well as from various philosophical and cultural studies' theories and methodologies. I will mention only a few additional aspects:

- Using mythology as anthropological insights into unconscious representations. I mentioned the myth of Oedipus, but others are of similar importance: for Freud, the myth of Narcissus; for Jacques Lacan, the myth of Antigone; and so on.
- Integrating poetic knowledge into psychoanalytic theory-building. Consider the importance the writer and dramatist Arthur Schnitzler had for Freud:

> Dear Dr. Schnitzler! For many years I have been conscious of the far-reaching conformity existing between your opinions and mine on many psychological and erotic problems; and recently I even found the courage expressly to emphasize this conformity ["Fragment of an Analysis of a Case of Hysteria", 1905]. I have

often asked myself in astonishment how you came by this or that piece of secret knowledge which I had acquired by a painstaking investigation of the subject, and I finally came to the point of envying the author whom hitherto I had admired. Now you may imagine how pleased and elated I felt on reading that you too have derived inspiration from my writings. I am almost sorry to think that I had to reach the age of fifty before hearing something so flattering. Yours in admiration, Dr. Freud.

(Freud, 1906)

Another example would be W. R. Bion, whose concept of "negative capability" is a quote from the poet Keats.

- Transduction of epistemological and interpretative concepts from cultural studies into psychoanalysis: Jacques Lacan (1953) adopted the linguistic theories of Ferdinand de Saussure for his theory of the significant, W. R. Bion (1962) used the term "reverie" brought forward by Charles Saunders Peirce to encompass his version of the analyst's free-floating attention. More recently, Ronald Britton (1998, pp. 166–196) referred to the poet William Blake, amongst others, to account for his concept of belief and imagination. Christopher Bollas (2013) has linked Chinese poetry to Winnicott's psychoanalytic praxis. I have mentioned here no more than a few examples for this work on translation.

In conclusion, transdisciplinary work is and should be a bidirectional dialogue that enables new insights to evolve via the dialogue instead of merely applying one side's concepts to the other side. In my view, transdisciplinary explorations can best be performed in a triangular discourse, meaning that bidirectional dialogue conjointly addresses a third object, topic, or issue, thus forming a triangle. This triangular discourse is not readily established because the topic or issue might be latent in the literature, for example, a novel or play, and it is a first interpretive step to state that this or that text can be fruitfully read under the heading of, say, a specific affect, a specific interpersonal constellation, and so on. Once this triangular field is spread out, the gains attained by the dialogue quickly come to light.

Transdisciplinary dialogue in a triangular field *in vivo*

Let me now point out which literary texts will be dealt with psychoanalytically and the topics I have chosen. The book starts with "Negativity and language in *King Lear*". The literary work is obviously the Shakespearean drama, and the perspective which serves as a point of departure for interpreting the text is the possibility of tolerating the negative or the experience of lack. The reason I have chosen this perspective is not only because of my theoretical preferences—in recent years, I have been working extensively with negative hermeneutics and negative anthropology as the basis of psychoanalytic thinking (Angehrn & Küchenhoff, 2013; Küchenhoff, 2013). My approach to the drama will be examining the ability to separate and the tolerance for loss and the negative in *King Lear* on three levels: the farewell to power in the process of growing older, the separation from the next generation, and the breakdown of a world view and handling the loss of social securities hitherto taken for granted. I then will add an analysis of the madness to which Lear succumbs—madness that is the consequence of a failure to deal constructively with loss and lack.

The narrative *Bartleby the Scrivener* by Herman Melville is discussed in the second chapter, entitled "On the chances and dead-ends of saying 'no'". Again, the topic is negativity, but the narrative deals with it in quite a different way, which was completely unusual for its time. I will show that withdrawal, rejection, or retreat from communication seem to describe a psychotic attitude, but a mere psychopathological point of view does not do justice to the text. Dealing with negative symptoms might be a major challenge for clinical therapeutic practice: is mutism, is the denial of communication or food, an expression of a loss of abilities, or does an understanding approach to such behavioural patterns enable one to find meaning in them? What Bartleby's negation of the other's demands has to say to the other remains open; whether it is a "no" by which someone destroys themselves or the other, or the contact between them, or whether the "no" entails a self-preservation, even self-assertion, as well—that is to be examined in each case in therapy.

In the third chapter, another text by Herman Melville, *Moby-Dick*, becomes the focus, and the topics chosen here are self-care and identity formation ("Aesthetic form and unconscious sense: self-care and identity in *Moby-Dick*"). The epistemological interest that guides the interpretation of *Moby-Dick* is the question of how self-care and self-destruction relate to processes of identity formation. First, I will explain the concept of self-care, and in a second step, I will give psychoanalytical aspects of self-care and self-destruction. Afterwards, the Melvillean concept as it is inherent to the novel's form will be made apparent.

The text sequence follows the chronology of publication dates. So, Chapter 4 addresses the novel *Embers* by Sándor Márai, written in English in the USA. The topic here is the analysis of the process of remembering. How remembering advances in the novel is comparable to the analytical situation in some respects. The past is reconstructed similarly, via conversation as a communicative setting, in which the guest is usually silent, and the host unfolds their memories, creating an asymmetrical dialogue situation. But there are obvious differences as well. Emotionality is lived out intensively, and a drama of love and death, of guilt and atonement, of perpetration and sacrifice evolves that is not worked through and ends in disaster.

Chapter 5 is concerned with "Intercultural violence and intercultural transitional spaces: construction and deconstruction of the foreign" and employs the novel *Tracks* by Louise Erdrich. This chapter is divided into three sections. The first part describes two corresponding mechanisms of border demarcation, the construction of the foreign and the construction of one's own identity, from a psychoanalytical perspective, with the aim of developing a concept that allows a critique of violence to formulate. The second part deals with complementary mechanisms, that is, questioning boundaries and thus preventing or overcoming violence. Of these, I use two metaphors crucial to psychoanalytic activity—the metaphor of transitional space and that of translation. In a concluding third part, I will describe the function of literary texts to create transcultural transitional spaces and to function as translating texts on the basis of the novel *Tracks*.

The following two chapters are devoted to small novels written by Philip Roth. Chapter 6 compares the process of dying in literature and psychoanalysis. Who can teach the art of dying? Is it literature, is it psychoanalysis? First, the retroactive nature of dying onto the life process or on one's own life story is characterised, and I exploit psychoanalytic and philosophical thoughts to find an answer to these important questions. Afterwards, the chapter compares and interprets two literary texts—two versions of the Everyman topic. These are the play with the same name, *Jedermann*, by Hugo von Hofmannsthal that is still presented each year at the Salzburg Summer Festival, and Philip Roth's novel *Everyman*.

Chapter 7 is concerned with the psychology of shame. It outlines an analysis of shame and its vicissitudes, and allows the novel to enrich the psychology of shame. First of all, it seems significant that shame is caused by physical suffering. Secondly, the text deals with a particularly shame-sensitive phase of life, late adolescence. Thirdly, the text allows for recognition of how important the other person is for the emergence and the consequences of shame, and that this holds true for generations; accordingly, the transgenerational aspect plays a significant role in the novel. The feeling of shame has its own history and its own "fate", that is, it is specifically processed and shapes the development of life history. In analogy to the term "vicissitude" concerning the fate of instincts, I will speak of the vicissitudes of shame to emphasise the biographical dynamics of shame. Finally, compared to other novels dealing with shame, *Nemesis* is much more pessimistic because it deals with the destructive power of shame if it is not integrated psychologically.

The topic in Chapter 8 is encounter and relationship in therapy and in everyday life. A therapeutic relationship refers to a specific therapeutic setting, and encounter, to an existential intersubjective communication. Therapy is characterised by an oscillation between encounter and relationship, understood in the sense just outlined. When we do therapy, we get involved with the people who come to us, we meet them as therapists. We allow the therapeutic sessions to be formed by our communication; we allow ourselves and our patients to develop together. And yet, the relationship between us remains asymmetrical; we use the encounter to draw conclusions that are explicitly more focused on the patient than on ourselves. We remain in a certain neutrality, and share much less of our personal history with the patient than the patient shares with us. On the other hand, we cannot work therapeutically with the relationship if we have not encountered each other. I will briefly introduce and discuss a contemporary novel which has rightly received the Man Booker Prize and is important for our topic. It is called *The Vegetarian* and was written by South Korean author Han Kang.

The theme of the concluding Chapter 9, "In transition: say goodbye and start over", is the transition from a farewell in the broadest sense, which includes separation, loss, and other similar experiences, to a new beginning that reopens the future. I thereby consider the three dimensions—farewell, transition, new beginning—under a time perspective. In the first part, which deals with farewells, the chapter highlights only one aspect of the many determinants of farewells: the great psychological difficulty of initiating and completing a farewell. In the second part, I examine the temporal characteristics of the transition between farewell and new beginning. Firstly, how long can or must a transition after a farewell be so that it can lead to a new beginning? Secondly, is the temporal relationship between farewell, transition, and new beginning to be understood as a consecutive sequence of events, or as repetitive and dynamically oscillating so that the sequence is passed through several times and repeatedly until it comes to an end? A third part examines the time structure of the new beginning. As a literary specimen, Nathan Hill's *The Nix* is interpreted along these lines, as the novel can be understood as a brilliant dispute on the chances of a goodbye to initiate a new start.

Closing this introduction, a personal remark seems appropriate. I have been engaged in transdisciplinary work from the outset of my psychoanalytic education. As I had the chance to study philosophy parallel to medicine (it would no longer be possible, at least not in Germany or Switzerland), philosophy seemed to be the most natural discipline to incorporate. As I always had a vivid interest in literature as well, I was happy to be elected as a member of the working party Psychoanalysis and Literature (www.litpsych.uni-freiburg.de/wp) in 2005, which has a scientific tradition of more than forty years in the field. As a personal preference, I read and worked on American and English literature with a particular passion. Some American psychoanalytic colleagues hit upon several publications hitherto only published in German, and they motivated me to collect my manuscripts on American and English literature, to have them translated, and thus to make them accessible to the English-speaking reader. I am grateful and much indebted to Phoenix Publishing House, and especially to its publisher Kate Pearce, for having supported and guided the publication project.

CHAPTER 1

Negativity and language in *King Lear* (W. Shakespeare)

Crises of separation are part of human life. They have to be mastered from the very beginning and remain challenges throughout life. This is a fundamental insight of psychoanalysis. What these challenges of separation consist of varies in the course of one's personal development.

The life of the infant begins with a first separation; there is no consensus on the significance of the so-called trauma of birth for the development of the personality (Houzel, 2005; Rank, 1929). In any case, birth is a prototype for those separations that necessarily arise at a point in time when it is not yet possible to actively deal with them and represent them, that is, to process them in thought. It is not yet possible to speak of the loss of an object, because there is no concept of an object, just as there is no concept of oneself, and thus the experience of loss is not yet a mentally represented experience—only a crisis-like increase of excitement. The experience of birth is not understood as the loss of an object; it is at most retrospectively interpreted as such. In later life, such unrepresentable experiences of loss may be repeated as traumas.

For many psychoanalytic authors, weaning is the first real experience of separation (Green, 1990; Grinberg & Grinberg, 1989), that is, an experience that is accompanied by feelings of loss and despair. It is connected with the sense of separation gradually appearing between the self and the other, at the same time as the emergence of an idea of the object. The child experiences a cut in the intercorporeity, the bodily "in-between" (Küchenhoff, 2012, pp. 54–58, 84–91) of mother's breast and his own mouth, he becomes aware that there are, on the one side, his own body or body zones as well as, on the other side, mother's body or body parts that escape his own control, that cannot be governed, that are obviously independent and belong to someone else. Already here the experience of separation has a double face: it allows the child to distinguish between partial aspects of self and object, at some point also between self and object as a whole, and to form a delimited self-image that is experienced as autonomous and, finally, an individual identity. Necessary though separations are for the development of personality, the experiences of loss and abandonment associated with them are just as painful. Julia Kristeva, who has worked intensively on cases of severe depression, posits their origin in the impossibility of going through the despair associated with initial separations, of "traversing" in her words: the separation must be experienced and endured, but must also be passed through (Kristeva, 1989, cf. Küchenhoff, 2013, Chapter 14).

Psychoanalytic developmental psychology assumes further early childhood separation experiences which are formative for personality development. The transition from a two-person to a three-person psychology is associated with the loss of the illusion that the most important caregivers are devoted only to one's own self, and with the realisation that the other person is committed to others as well: there is not only the self and the object, but also the third, the fourth, the fifth. And these relationships elude one's own control. It is not easy to bear this. Freud uses a striking term to characterise the child's painful feeling of being separated from both parents and thus being excluded. He speaks of the "primal scene", the origin of all scenes. The child, who is the core of the primal scene experience, becomes aware that the parents have a passionate relationship with each other in which he has no direct involvement. The primal scene stands for the original introduction to triangulation. The recognition of the relationship that the loved ones have with others remains a crucial developmental task throughout life. The recognition of the parents' love relationship is rightly considered one of the facts of life to be accepted (Money-Kyrle, 1978). The child does not come into the world with "triadic competence" (Bürgin & von Klitzing, 2001), instead he has to build it up, that is, to be prepared to acknowledge the complex triangular reality and to use it. The ability to deal with separations entailing the loss connected to them will be challenged throughout life.

Deliberately, these remarks are chosen as a starting point because I want to discuss the drama *King Lear* by Shakespeare from the point of view of the experience of separation and tolerance of the negative and lack. The reason I chose this perspective is not only because of my theoretical preferences—in recent years, I have been working a lot with negative hermeneutics and negative anthropology as the basis of psychoanalytic thinking (Angehrn & Küchenhoff, 2013; Küchenhoff, 2013). Certainly, personal motives also played a role when I first wrote this chapter. I was concerned with questions of personal and social development linked to loss and mourning, as I was about to end my career as the medical director of a large psychiatric centre. I was confronted with the challenges of letting go, being able to hand over the institutions I had built up, and I had to ask myself what could cause a failure in meeting these challenges. Similar challenges held true in my family. So I had to ask myself: how well do I manage, having not three daughters like King Lear, but two, not to hinder them in their own development and life expectancies and not to bind them by false and egocentric love? On the contrary, what is to be preserved and not given away in a time when we cannot help but perceive the violation of democratic values, that manipulation and marketing tricks are more successful than honesty? The word "postfactual" is as stupid as it is accurate: it highlights the recklessness of people who are concerned with power but not with the common good and who are unfortunately successful with it; it is a stupid word because there can, of course, be nothing postfactual.

The Shakespearean drama has upset and continues to upset me in these three respects. Such personal involvement should not be misunderstood as an impediment to access the drama. Generally speaking, the act of reading (or attending a performance on stage) should and does include being stirred up, being questioned, being touched. My personal thoughts show that the aesthetic response as part of the "process between text and reader" has quickly taken hold of me (Iser, 1980,

p. 85). So, reacting personally to the text opens up and sharpens the understanding, but it certainly precludes consideration of other contexts as well. Anyway, my approach to the drama will be examining the ability to separate and the tolerance for loss and the negative in *King Lear* on the three levels already introduced: the farewell to power in the process of growing older, the separation from the next generation, the breakdown of a world view and the handling of the loss of social securities hitherto taken for granted. The levels do not contradict each other but comment on each other. I then will add an analysis of the madness into which Lear slides. Madness is the product and consequence of a failure to deal constructively with loss and lack. What is special about the drama, however, is that inherent in the madness, sparks of a productive new beginning appear in a play that otherwise ends disastrously.

On the difficulties in dealing with *King Lear*

It is difficult to add anything original to the immense flood of texts published on *King Lear*. For the years between 2000 and 2009, the international bibliography of the Modern Language Association, the MLA Database (www.mla.org/Publications/MLA-International-Bibliography), lists 548 articles; in the previous decade, there were 635 articles and 194 books (Kelly, 2011, p. 78). Moreover, it is almost impossible to process even a rudimentary part of this secondary literature.

In addition, we are confronted with another difficulty: what are we dealing with when we want to deal with the Shakespearean text of *King Lear*? For there *is* no canonical text to which all dramaturges or critics could refer. The first print dates from 1608, *True Chronicle History of King Leir*, the so-called First Quarto text. It was from this text that the King's Men, the theatre company in which Shakespeare also participated, started their performances at the Globe Theatre and many other venues (Wells, 2000). Through performing, the play changed, was supplemented, and the text was rewritten in some parts. These revisions were summarised seven years after Shakespeare's death, and in 1623 the so-called First Folio—an edition of the *Collected Works*—was produced. From 1723 onwards, Alexander Pope re-edited the *Collected Works*, he compiled the Quarto and Folio into a new integrated text, and this tradition was maintained until the mid-1980s. Only then was it recognised that each of the two texts formed an independent version of the play, and both appeared in the Complete Edition, *The New Oxford Shakespeare*. In the following I will refer to the version edited by Stanley Wells, which reproduces the Quarto text (Shakespeare, 2000).

A further difficulty arises when it comes to paying tribute to Shakespeare's genuine achievement. Namely, he did not invent the material. In 1605, a play was published anonymously, called *The True Chronicle of King Leir and His Three Daughters Gonorill, Regan and Cordella*. The publication seems to date back to a play first performed in 1594. But even in this work, the story was not original. Rather, as a legend, it belongs to the stock of cultural knowledge of the time. In the twelfth century, the story appears in the *Historia Regum Britanniae*, although it has no secure historical basis. In the *Genealogy of the Kings of England* of 1560, the story appears again, as well as in 1577 in the *History of England*. Finally, among the many sources that are by no means exhaustively reproduced here, the most important is the *Arcadia* romance by Sir Philip Sidney, published in 1590, which contains numerous motifs that recur in Shakespeare's *King Lear*. So, when we look at the Shakespearean drama, it is not enough to offer an interpretation of the material, which in its basic form does not originate in Shakespeare. Nevertheless, we may appreciate his specific and unique processing of the material (all information by Wells, 2000).

One last obstacle is yet to be named: the influence of theatre practice on the content. The play is influenced by the performance habits that had developed in the Shakespearean theatre. Since the King's Men not only performed in the Globe Theatre, but also spent significant time on the road, stage props were apparently largely dispensed with. The surviving text is not divided into acts and scenes. (This division is a later addition and must be viewed critically.) This fact alone opens up a wide scope for interpretation. All roles were played by men and boys—women had no access to acting. Astonishingly often, letters are negotiated in the play—they serve to structure the spoken text and are thus a dramaturgical trick (Kelly, 2011, p. 86).

On ageing and its challenges

Lear is at the end of his life, he is—as can be calculated from some remarks—eighty years old. Therefore, he wants to hand over his power and dominion to his three daughters, Regan, Goneril, and Cordelia.

It is, of course, questionable whether he really wants this and whether he is capable of acting accordingly. The drama's conflict is fuelled by the way in which the king chooses to process the handover. He conducts a love test: the daughters are to describe their love to their father. In this way, Lear wants to secure the love of the daughters so that they remain united with and loyal to him. This is a very sensitive moment for Lear—he renounces his power, but he wants guarantees. He forces a precarious exchange on his daughters: power and money for affection. What should he build on when he steps down? He relies, above all, on the fact that there is a bond of love that binds him to his daughters, which guarantees him security and respect. But this means that where he renounces, he binds at the same time.

What is demanded of the daughters are words. Language acts as a mediator between the disparate variables of power and affection. The two older sisters use language strategically. They exaggerate their vows of love in order to receive as much of the inheritance as possible. They use language entirely in the service of power; the psychological aspect, the attitude towards the father, is conjured up in words, but it does not play an honest role. Speech is subordinated to political interest, and in terms of personal relationships, it is dishonest. Cordelia, on the other hand, distrusts words, she chooses the simplest possible form of expression and avoids any hyperbole, yet she has fundamental doubts about the mediating function of language. Right at the beginning of the problematic game, she asks herself: "What can I do?" and gives herself the answer: "Love and be silent" (1.57).[1] "I cannot heave / My heart into my mouth", she says a little later (1.83–4). Kent, who stands up for her and urges Lear to reverse his decision to disinherit Cordelia, emphasises that it is the effects of language and the deeds associated with words that produce truth: "And your large speeches may approve your deeds, / That good effects may spring from words of love" (1.174–175)—these words are directed to the other two sisters who use tactics.

So, Cordelia does not reject the father, but rather his test. She cannot imagine that language can really mediate between power and feeling. Words are used to achieve a strategic goal and therefore cannot

---

[1] Quotes according to William Shakespeare (2000); first number: scene, second number: line.

name emotional attitudes. Besides Kent, Cordelia is the only one who understands language as the bearer of a symbolic order. For she soberly and extremely succinctly, but just as clearly, identifies the mutual bond that she and her father have as a reliable bond. She does not narcissistically abuse language by using it to satisfy imaginary desires. In this way, she clearly distinguishes herself from her father. She does not want to satisfy his narcissism, but she wants to show how steadfast their mutual relationship is. She chooses her words carefully to preserve their emotionality, a semiotic quality that resonates in the words. "Nor are those empty-hearted whose low sound / Reverbs no hollowness"—so says Kent (1.144–145). This is a beautiful and intense image: the soft sound that a person strikes refers to the density of his or her feeling—if this were hollow, the sound would vibrate loudly, but be meaningless, without substance. The loud sound of the sisters refers, in reverse, to their hollowness. An acoustic metaphor is used for Cordelia's straightness.

Lear hears only personal disregard in the quiet tone Cordelia strikes and is deeply offended by the recognisable demarcation of his favourite daughter, who wants to affirm a symbolic, not imaginary, bond with her father. Cordelia's disinheritance, the shaming and condemnation of the favourite daughter, are a prime example of narcissistic rage. The *quid pro quo* fails. He apparently did not just want to achieve contractual security through the love test, but to make an exchange: I give you political power and money, and you give me back the recognition I need for myself. He cannot fathom the loyalty inherent in Cordelia's words. Instead, he remains—old man that he is, just giving up his profession of being king—dependent on narcissistic reflection. He seeks confirmation in the image, in the imaginary, and he cannot bear the danger of not mirroring himself in the proclaimed love of his daughters. The fear of being or becoming worthless and superfluous when he is no longer king weighs too heavily.

The impossibility to really give up power is evident again, now in reference to the daughters Regan and Goneril, who have received Cordelia's share and who have promised to take care of their father in turn. What the text does not say, but what the audience of the time certainly knew: since 1601 there had been a decree in the English kingdom (Poor Law Act) which obliged relatives to provide for their old parents. Lear cannot let loose—he has renounced the task of being king, and yet he claims for himself, as it were in a clause, the insignia of ruler and a troop of at least a hundred knights. (How would this have been received if Benedict XVI had combined his resignation as pope with the claim to have a dozen cardinals at his own disposal?) Lear wants to pass his power on, but he cannot really break away from it. The path he has chosen, the test of love as well as the clause of domination, creates the suffering that will prove fatal as the tragedy progresses. Lear's madness will once again confirm in an impressive way how much he has remained king in his own imagination, how impossible it is for him to renounce dominion and its insignia.

On the double difficulty of letting the next generation go and saying goodbye to parents

It might already have become evident in the depictions of the previous section what the children, the daughters, should represent for the father. In psychoanalytical theory, narcissism stands for this tendency, which has probably been best described by André Green (1983), in its at least threefold form: as *libidinal* narcissism demanding of the other, of the object, to be and behave exactly as it conforms to the self's own aspirations; as narcissism of *the One*, in which there are only followers or opponents, pillars stabilising the self or enemies endangering the self, and where the object functions as a decal of the self; as narcissism of *the None*, in which unity is produced only by destroying all differences, and often enough also the persons who represent these differences. This latter narcissism is identical with destructive narcissism. The daughters apparently serve Lear as a narcissistic prolongation; they serve to satisfy a narcissism of the One: as persons, they have no independent meaning, they serve the father only to maintain the self-image. And not only that: for Lear, they should be "guardians" and "depositaries" (7.409).

All the daughters refuse this role; the two older ones, of course, only after they have been given power by their father. They set limits to him by finally evading the father's desire for the narcissistic confirmation they had previously given him. But unlike many interpreters, I do not see in this a successful separation and detachment. For both elder daughters remain caught up in the narcissistic relationship. In humiliating and embarrassing their father, they show that they have not gained any distance from or a symbolically mediated relationship with him. The humiliation is made drastically obvious through the gradual decimation of his entourage: Lear initially has a hundred knights to accompany him, Gonoril halves them, Regan halves them again, to twenty-five, and finally prohibits any accompaniment. The text makes it abundantly clear in the immediately following lines that Lear perceives this act as a castration. He emphasises that he could burst with anger and go mad, but that he will not cry "unmanly" like a woman. (See also 20.110ff.: Here, Lear spreads about sexual themes: "Let copulation thrive" and so on, only to add a few lines later—apparently abruptly— "for I lack soldiers". The incoherent text, while appearing fragmented from psychosis, reveals its very precise meaning through this addition.)

Even Cordelia, as we have seen, does not mirror her father's need for narcissistic reassurance. Instead of offering an imaginary one, she suggests a real, symbolically based relationship; but Lear is not in a position to realise this. Yet in a certain sense, Cordelia seems to be similar to her father in a particular form of blindness. She obviously must have known him and his vanity, even his irascibility. She should be able to guess what the father desires to hear. She does not do him the favour of satisfying his narcissism. By taking an emancipative step, through which she frees herself from the narcissistic bondage, Cordelia, the favourite daughter, is herself wreaking havoc that unfolds in the further course of the piece. Her sisters delimit themselves superficially, but they do not emancipate themselves. Rather, they only take revenge. This revenge may give satisfaction, as it is directed against the fatherly abuse of the children. But it remains caught up in the narcissism of the narcissistic One. Once their father has fallen out of their childish idealisation, they inflict upon him the utmost shame, which has been described as castration (see below, "Sexualisation in delusion"). Again, the revenge and humiliation are made very obvious: Lear is left without protection in the storm, the wind and weather. "To wilful men / The injuries that they themselves procure / Must be their schoolmasters" (8.459–460), Regan comments on this murderous decision not to give the father any more accommodation.

The text tells little about the further fate of Cordelia. Although disinherited, she is later on married to the king of France—Lear had handed her over to him like a worthless commodity. Only at the end of the play does she reappear, but then dies quickly by a hired murderer. She is taken prisoner after losing the war on the side of France and killed in the dungeon by an order from Edmund, the illegitimate child of the Earl of Gloucester. It remains unclear why she, who was considered the "better soldier" shortly before, loses the war. It seems as if she is weakened by the re-encounter with her father. The play does not report on how the war develops. In any case, Edmund wins, France is subjugated, and Lear and Cordelia, the queen of France, are taken prisoner.

Lear's touching declaration of love to his daughter (24.9–13): "We two alone will sing like birds i'th' cage. / … / And pray, and sing, and tell old tales, and laugh / At gilded butterflies", wonderfully formulated as it is, is the last conversation between father and daughter. Together they go to prison, and Lear's imaginary thinking changes the imprisonment eventually leading to his death into a song of birds; he certainly is in a cage, but in reality, he is left completely alone there. It is touching to watch how his affectionate love for his daughter breaks through with great élan—a magnificent portrayal of love–death, in this case a love–death of father and daughter, thus bearing an incestuous note! Lear knows that he is being held in prison, and does not in any way misunderstand the situation, but he again allows affect, this time the love affect, to take precedence over the sober assessment of a hopeless situation. In this situation, he seeks forgiveness from his daughter, just as she had asked for his blessing in the first reunion. If we assume that Cordelia shares the feelings inherent in her father's declaration of love, and so Lear does not say something displeasing, and assuming that she is in agreement with him, then in the end she would have returned to his arms, and would have taken back her steps to separation. Is that why she also failed militarily? Edmund, who has the upper hand in war, without winning or surviving in the end, declares in another scene, without reference to Cordelia: "To be tender-minded / Does not become a sword" (24.31f.). Nevertheless, this statement allows one to understand her military failure: Cordelia's regression in the face of her father makes her lose her sword, as it were.

The very moment she sees her father in his misery, she gives up demanding a symbolically mediated relationship and thus, finally, adopts an imaginary position towards him. Although she seeks the doctor who is supposed to help Lear, she sees herself as a doctor—and again, there is evidence of an incestuous love affair:

O my dear father, restoration hang
Thy medicine on my lips, and let this kiss
Repair those violent harms that my two sisters
Have in thy reverence made!

(21.24–27)

Here, Cordelia submits to a great and narcissistic hubris, maintaining that a kiss of the loving daughter can save the father. In this moment, Cordelia puts aside all other feelings towards her father, and even seems to forget how he dropped her in the worst way possible. Instead, she redirects her thoughts to her father's conflict with her sisters. She does not reflect on what she herself has contributed to the deadly development of the family by offending the father.

Lear is thus a play that shows that the children fail to separate and become autonomous if narcissistic cathexis by the father is not taken back. In the end, narcissism of the One turns into a destructive narcissism that leads to death for all.

There is a blank space in the Lears' family drama. There is a person who is not spoken of: it is Lear's wife, the mother of the three daughters, if they had the same mother at all. In any case, there is no woman at Lear's side. Lear's cruel curses against his daughters contain many passages contemptuous of women. Thus, the oedipal third in the family structure is missing. With Lacan, we know that the order of the personal third can also be guaranteed by the symbolic order of a contract, of a mutual recognition of the positions one takes in relation to one another. In this respect, the third party or the third is introduced, or at least conjured up, right at the beginning of the drama by Cordelia's invocation of the symbolic order—of the bond that connects father and daughter without being absorbed in the imaginary narcissistic wish fulfilment. The figure of Kent, who preserves his contract with Lear till the end, stands for this quiet hope that the symbolic order can be maintained after all. This is how I understand Kent's remarks, which would otherwise sound ambiguous: when Albany, Goneril's husband, speaks admonishing words at the end, Kent leaves the scene, arguing that he still has some obligations to fulfil. In this way, he exposes Albany's grand closing words as a sham; they are unbelievable because Albany had by no means taken a clear position.

I am not the only one to realise that Queen Lear is missing in the play. Gordon Bottomly, a writer who has remained largely unknown, published a one-act play in 1916, entitled *King Lear's Wife*, which describes the queen's last hours: while she is lying in bed seriously ill, Lear has engaged beautiful young women as nurses, supposedly because young life would help his wife to recover, but in reality, with the intention to seduce them. Thus, he lures a guard away from her bed into his own, with the corollary that the queen dies in the meantime. Goneril, realising what has happened, stabs the guard. In this way, the drama continues. Obviously, this mediocre play (which at least—and not quite awkwardly—tries to copy the verse measure used by Shakespeare) was written out of the need to construct a family history in the bourgeois age, surely also in order to finally lay all blame on the king. It is no wonder that the daughters do not forgive him for murdering his wife and their mother. Incidentally, all secondary literature shows a strong tendency to take sides.

The failure of separation, intolerance of the negative and lack, and the productive negativity of insanity

What does the play reveal in terms of the triggers and causes of insanity?

Early on, the two older daughters summarise the factors that could endanger the father: age, a lack of self-knowledge ("yet he hath ever but slenderly known himself"; 1.280f.), a particular personality ("the imperfection of long-engrafted condition"; 1.287), a choleric temperament, and finally, illness ("unruly waywardness that infirm and choleric years bring with them"; 1.288f.). Cordelia describes Lear's condition, when he finally goes insane, as "untuned and hurrying senses" (21.14), and that she has a father who is "child-changed" (21.15)—a brilliant formulation, for it is ambiguous. The father has become a child, yes, but at the same time, the father has been changed by his child or children. Thus, the delusion has to do with childishness—with regression. But it also stems from the traumatising relationships. This unusual and striking word "child-changed" entails this double meaning! Albany had already accused the daughters Goneril and Regan of having driven their father crazy: "A father ... have you madded" (16.40–42). For Shakespeare and his contemporaries, there was a possibility of driving someone mad.

How does Lear's delusion develop?

In Scene 4, Goneril devalues Lear, who lives with her, and Lear begins to doubt his mental state. Goneril does not narcissistically reflect him, she harasses him, and Lear feels threatened in his psychological integrity: "Who is it that can tell me who I am?" (4.225). On the one hand, these words address all the others ignoring his dignity, not remembering that it is the king himself with whom they are actually dealing. But on the other hand, Lear actually addresses himself and shows his severe self-doubts. It is precisely at this point that Lear loses control of language for the first time, and he briefly speaks a few incoherent sentences:

> We that too late repent's—o sir, are you come? [Albany has entered the stage]
> Is it your will that we—prepare my horses.
>
> (4.249–250)

He notices the turmoil himself a short time later:

> … O Lear, Lear!
> Beat at that gate [sc. his head] that let thy folly in
> And thy dear judgment out. …
>
> (4.262–263)

Immediately after that, however, he pulls himself together, stabilises himself, and restores his expressiveness by screaming a curse on Goneril. Similarly destructive curses can hardly ever be found in literature. But language has regained its order—an impressive testimony to how narcissistic rage stabilises the personality structure in that it can direct the intention to the despised object and push away all self-doubt. The narcissistic anger stabilises the structure. Lear reflects on regaining psychic structure:

> … I'll resume the shape which thou dost think
> I have cast off for ever …
>
> (4.300–301)

Scenes 9–11 are central to the dramatic plot: Lear is in the middle of a storm, but he does not want to enter the house to protect himself. His narcissism has now taken hold of the world, and he identifies with the storm and wishes the whole world to perish—a world that has been lost to him through his daughters' betrayal. As an answer, Lear equates historic time and his personal lifetime, as is characteristic of a totalitarian leader (Blumenberg, 1986). As a sequela of his narcissism, Lear no longer takes the otherness of the other into account; although he hears Edgar detailing his own misery, Lear can only and exclusively imagine that he too has been betrayed by his daughters.

Lear himself notices that he gradually goes crazy: "My wit begins to turn" (9.68). Immediately after this insight, he turns empathetically to his fool, who always accompanies him: "Come on, my boy. How dost, my boy? Art cold?" (9.69). Such words from Lear's mouth are surprising, for at this point and for the first time, he asks someone else about his feelings, at least for a short while, instead of reducing the other to a narcissistic decal. A little later, he even develops compassion for all his subjects, who are much more exposed to the rigours of the weather, and so on, and he has self-critical thoughts about his exercise of power:

> Poor naked wretches, wheresoe'er you are,
> That bide the pelting of this pitiless night,
> How shall your houseless heads and unfed sides,
> Your looped and windowed raggedness, defend you
> From seasons such as these? O, I have ta'en
> Too little care of this …
>
> (11.25–30)

This is an important turning point; it signals no less than the fact that madness can offer a widened horizon and a new knowledge. While in mental distress, Lear is able to grasp the misery of others, and only then, when he no longer fights against his crisis with appeals for manliness and such self-excitement, he accepts it. In other words, only in the psychotic experience—in the delusional misjudgement of his surroundings—can he overcome his destructive narcissism.

The transition from narcissistic mania to madness is magnificently portrayed in the scene in which Lear holds a bogus court session with Edgar, Kent, and the jester (13.31ff.). The court is made up of Lear, Kent in disguise, Edgar, the legitimate son of Gloucester and Edmund's brother, who plays a mentally ill man from the Bedlam asylum, and the jester. It is touching to watch Lear talk to Edgar, whom he regards as a philosopher, as his own kind. The jester fully understands how the world is functioning, and he only wraps the truth in the jester's garb. Edgar disguises himself as an inmate of Bedlam to escape persecution, and Lear indeed goes mad. Thus, a remarkable gathering takes place on the stage: the one who, through the jester's garb, protects himself from persecution (Edgar), the one who has always taken the role of fool to be able to speak the truth (the jester), the persecuted one, the only one untouched by this madness, but who has also disguised himself because he is politically persecuted (Kent). They gather because they have to judge Lear's daughters and condemn them. In the end, they suggest that Regan be dissected to see what her heart looks like—a heart that can breed such bad behaviour.

In the following, Lear loses his mind completely, walks around with a crown of leaves, tears his clothes off, and sings. He obviously does not suffer in the same way as before. His language decays, and he no longer speaks in verse alone, but also in prose, switching back and forth arbitrarily between the two. The language seems to be worldly and disintegrated (in conversation with Edgar, see 20.86ff., or in conversation with Gloucester in the same scene, 106ff.).

Gloucester expresses what the function of delusion is:

> ... Better I were distraught;
> So should my thoughts be fencèd from my griefs,
> And woes by wrong imagination lose
> The knowledge of themselves.
>
> (20.274–277)

So, the delusion has a protective effect. It protects against grief and despair: thoughts are freed from feelings which would otherwise impose themselves on the subject and become overwhelming. It is only when the madness subsides and the old and new pain overwhelms the subject that it can break one's heart: that is what Gloucester dies of, and that is what Lear dies of at the end of the piece. The doctor had prescribed rest, music, and the presence of loved ones as remedies. That Lear is finally confronted with the death of his daughter turns out to overwhelm him. But then he is no longer insane.

Delusion may present wishes as fulfilled; this is expressed very clearly in the play. Once enclosed in a delusion, Lear no longer rages and is more balanced. In delusion, Lear claims to still be installed in his political function: "I am the King himself" (20.83). In madness, it becomes clear how impossible it is for Lear to renounce this. In the pseudo-forensic scene already described, Lear exerts jurisdiction, as it is the prerogative of a king in his own subjective conviction: being mad allows him to judge. Thus, he acquits Gloucester, who kneels before him: "I pardon that man's life" (20.107).

Besides this wish fulfilment, delusion opens up a new ability to intuit and observe. In delusion, Lear can be more clairvoyant than ever before, as far as daughters are concerned: "To say 'ay' and 'no' to everything I said and 'ay' and 'no' to was no good divinity" (20.98f.).

As Freud (1911c) has pointed out in his seminal paper on Daniel Paul Schreber, delusion allows the rise of a (new) world, rearranging thoughts that have been disturbed. In this way, it enables precise observations and insights that were previously subdued.

It is essential, however, that Lear is only able to recognise himself and others correctly in delusion—foremost, his own failure. The literary scholar Peter von Matt is certainly right when he writes: "Only in real madness does the truth dawn upon him, he reaches the edge of reason" (Matt, 1995, p. 158). Delusion and reason then turn sides. As it were, in delusion there is more reason than in the rigid adherence to the traditional roles and functions that only prevent offence. Delusion is the prerequisite for empathy and engenders knowledge and self-criticism. So, there could be hope in the course of the play. Lear could find a new start, but Shakespeare does not allow a happy end. Instead, the narcissistic, symbiotic, and incestuous desire takes over again as soon as the delusion subsides. Lear feels happy in prison because he is united with his favourite daughter. He can no longer recognise the truth once he has recovered from the delusion. This is a very modern view of psychosis that I share: there is not only a destructive but also a productive negativity in psychotic experience (Küchenhoff, 2018).

What is there to hope for in the end? Is Kent a source of hope? At least, he survives and—as we had pointed out—he supports the symbolic order, but on the other hand, he cannot influence the evolution of the tragedy. It will be difficult to find any position of hope in a decidedly gloomy end, when almost everyone, "good" or "evil", perishes. Edgar survives, protected by feigned madness. The most potent resource of hope, and this would be an even more radical interpretation, is madness itself. In madness, there is a power and a chance to realise the breakdown, and also to represent it, thus opening up an opportunity to become aware of the disaster and perhaps find a way out.

The loss of ideologies

The play is obviously written in England at the beginning of the seventeenth century. Even though the plot is deliberately timeless (when the play is set remains unclear—a pagan culture is essentially presupposed, but even this attribution of time remains contradictory, namely when Edgar is introduced as Lear's godchild), it is clear that it deals with political issues of the time: dynastic succession, power struggles in the transfer of power, the exclusion of illegitimate children, to name but a few. The anthropological or supra-temporal psychological interpretation that we have provided so far immediately exposes itself to the accusation of ripping the piece out of its historical context and thus neglecting an essential intention of the text, misunderstanding its content by decontextualising it.

This supposition shall be dealt with at the end of this chapter. In the introduction, I noted three levels of interpretation which do not exclude but rather enhance each other. Now the social aspect is to be added; it will be shown that the experiences of the ageing king's loss of power and the family conflicts are embedded in a social dynamic that places the piece in its historical context, but which, on the other hand, is topical in a surprising way so that it is still relevant.

In this respect, one parallel action, which has not been mentioned before, must be briefly touched upon: the Earl of Gloucester has two sons, but like Lear, no partner at his side; the sons are called Edmund and Edgar. Edmund has the disadvantage of illegitimate birth, which is not his fault but nevertheless imposes social barriers on him. Edgar is the son born in wedlock and therefore preferred. Now Edmund defends himself against his fate by instigating an intrigue: he insinuates that his brother Edgar has murderous intentions to get rid of his father, whereas, in reality, it is his own wish. He denunciates Edgar to the father in a dramaturgically effective manner, who—acting as abruptly and angrily as Lear—condemns the favourite son. The latter hides under the mask of Tom of Bedlam, a mentally ill person who once was interned and now is set free again. Edmund pushes the brother aside and seduces Lear's elder daughters, Regan and Goneril, to both fall in love with him, with the foreseeable effect that they fight each other and finally die—one by the hand of the other, who then lays hands on herself. Gloucester, the father, is blinded and lives on in the play as a blind man, only to die in the end, not by suicide, as he wants, but by a broken heart.

But it is not the psychological dimension (which in itself is of psychodynamic interest because of the blinding motif) that will be our focus now, rather the figure of the villain, who is not only the villain, but also the one who proclaims a new ideology in which he believes, and which is completely different from the conventional order:

> Thou, nature, art my goddess; to thy law
> My services are bound. Wherefore should I
> Stand in the plague of custom and permit
> The curiosity of nations to deprive me,
> For that I am some twelve or fourteen moonshines
> Lag of a brother? Why "bastard"? Wherefore "base"?
> When my dimensions are as well compact,
> My mind as generous, and my shape as true,
> As honest madam's issue?
> Why brand they us with "base, base Bastardy"? Who in the lusty
> stealth of nature take
> More composition and fierce quality
> Than doth within a stale, dull-eyed bed go
> To the creating a whole tribe of fops,
> Got 'tween asleep and wake? Well then,
> Legitimate Edgar, I must have your land:
> Our father's love is to the bastard Edmund
> As to the legitimate.
> Well, my legitimate, if
> This letter speed and my invention thrive,
> Edmund the base shall to th' legitimate.
> I grow; I prosper. Now, gods, stand up for bastards!
>
> (2.1–21)

Edmund does not accept that he be locked up in any tradition, and sharply criticises a legal system that denies rights to those born out of wedlock. In this monologue, he reflects on the meaning of the word "legitimate". Peter von Matt (1995), who has given us a wonderful interpretation of this passage, emphasises that Edmund causes the traditional order to collapse by realising that words can be changed, that the signifier is no longer strictly bound to the signified, but can be exchanged, and so can the seemingly natural conditions be revealed as arbitrary distributions. Therefore, the order of who is or is not the real offspring can be reversed.

A short time later, he and his father each have a monologue, entirely in prose, in which the incompatibility of world views is once again made immediately clear. Gloucester says:

> These late eclipses in the sun and moon portend no good to us: though the wisdom of nature can reason it thus and thus, yet nature finds itself scourged by the sequent effects: love cools, friendship falls off, brothers divide: in cities, mutinies; in countries, discord; in palaces, treason; and the bond cracked 'twixt son and father. This villain of mine comes under the prediction; there's son against father: the king falls from bias of nature; there's father against child. We have seen the best of our time: machinations, hollowness, treachery, and all ruinous disorders, follow us disquietly to our graves. Find out this villain, Edmund; it shall lose thee nothing; do it carefully. And the noble and true-hearted Kent banished! His offence, honesty! 'Tis strange.
>
> (2.101–109)

This could have also come from Lear: the old-world view, according to which the accustomed order remains stable, is no longer correct. But Gloucester has no answer to this, for he experiences this collapse of order as catastrophic and fateful. He continues to rely on the old patterns of interpretation in order to be able to understand the changed and highly stressful circumstances around him: It's all in the stars, and the good times are behind us.

The son is different, who immediately afterwards answers in his monologue, without the father hearing it:

This is the excellent foppery of the world, that, when we are sick in
fortune, often the surfeit of our own behavior, we make guilty of
our disasters the sun, the moon, and the stars: as if we were villains
by necessity; fools by heavenly compulsion; knaves, thieves, and
treachers, by spherical predominance; drunkards, liars, and adul-
terers, by an enforced obedience of planetary influence; and all
that we are evil in, by a divine thrusting on: an admirable evasion
of whoremaster man, to lay his goatish disposition to the charge of
a star! My father compounded with my mother under the dragon's
tail; and my nativity was under Ursa major; so that it follows, I am
rough and lecherous. But, I should have been that I am, had the
maidenliest star in the firmament twinkled on my bastardy.

(2.110–124)

No, Edmund knows that the old order no longer works and that it is up
to the people to redesign it. Edmund is the radically enlightened person
in the guise of the villain (Matt, 1995, p. 152ff.); he resists a social system
built on injustice and pretending to be born of divine wisdom. "Let me,
if not by birth, have land by wit" (2.170), he says right at the beginning of
the drama. That is what it is all about: cunning takes the place of birth-
right. In the Folio version, Edmund reflects on the word "legitimate"
during his monologue, "fine word: legitimate" (2.18). Edmund questions the concepts, he emphasises that legitimacy is not God-given, that
classifications can be questioned, as it were at will, and everything can
become the starting point for criticism. The critique of language is the
root of social criticism. In the monologues of Gloucester and Edmund,
which are both of exactly the same length, there is an historical clash:
the Middle Ages of God-given principles of order suddenly meet the lib-
erated modern age (Matt, 1995, p. 151). Edmund embodies the modern
man who has cast off all traditional ties. Lear, on the other hand, like
Gloucester, cannot help but feel that he is the centre of a sacred order
based on reliable and unquestionable structures, which is always legiti-
mised. Now, however, it is collapsing, and Lear must realise for himself
that this order was not natural, but rather, it was only the effect of language. To repeat once more: "Only in real madness does the truth dawn
upon him, he reaches the edge of reason" (Matt, 1995, p. 158).

In the drama *King Lear*, an epochal change is negotiated. It is a drama of transition, but also of failed transition, of decay—of the old order, without a new one already visible. At best, a different order is hinted at by Cordelia's and Kent's different use of language. This is the third negativity that of course is connected with the negativities of age and family conflict: in a theatre play of the early modern period, change in world views is processed as the replacement of the theocentric and absolutist world view by one of enlightenment and criticism. At the same time, it also shows that the modern era might encounter new conflicts, for example, by the seizing of individual power through the dissolution of conventional ties. The psychological and political dimensions interpenetrate each other, as the narcissism of personality corresponds to the one-dimensionality of the ruler, who has no capacity for self-reflection and can only realise via the failure of his power that he has abused it by exploiting it beyond measure.

I am convinced that this is precisely the reason why *King Lear* still means so much to us today. It opens a double perspective, exploring in one and the same piece social systems as well as individuals who cannot change, who can no longer meet the demands placed on them, who are no longer able to reflect and critically question themselves. The personal level reflects the social level and vice versa. Today, we are confronted with the loss of reliable and value-based social rules and regulations as well. *King Lear* is modern and up to date, as a piece of transition, of epochal change, of transgenerational disparities.

Conclusion: hope and poetry

The drama does not convey much hope. The protagonists who represent the new world, such as Edmund, are so corrupt that the spectator cannot identify with them any more than with Lear's elder daughters. If anyone does, Cordelia and Kent offer a little bit of hope. As a writer, Shakespeare works on and with language. Only language or the form of speaking conveys hope. Lear's language expressing the old order decays; this loss of language engenders new expressive potentialities, especially the ability for self-criticism. Edmund belongs to the new order that is looming on the horizon. He plays with language, and thus is able to lie—and he does so constantly. The language of Cordelia and Kent is direct, simple, straightforward. When Kent says:

> To be acknowledged, madam, is o'erpaid
> All my reports go with the modest truth
> No more, nor clipped, but so.
>
> (20.3–5)

This applies to both. Albany's concluding words are dedicated to language: "Speak what we feel not what we ought to say" (24.319).

What hopes do we have, in a world order that is changing rapidly, where right-wing extremism is resurgent seventy-five years after the Nazi terror in Germany, where presidents are turning into dictators before our eyes, where elections are manipulated by hacker attacks, where the fifth commandment apparently no longer applies, when terrorism so shamelessly slaughters people? Are we finding the right language that allows us to respond to the challenges of our present time? Do we bury ourselves in the narcissism of the traditional? Do we adapt, do we make economic gains from the disasters of the present, such as the conditions in the countries from which refugees reach us? Are we beneficiaries of the misery of others?

The catastrophic end of the drama *King Lear* makes me think of Brecht's last lines of *The Good Person of Sezuan*: "Ladies and gentlemen, in you we trust: There must be happy endings, must, must, must!" (Brecht & Bentley, 1965).

In other words, even if the end can be read conservatively and has repeatedly been understood as the downfall of the villains and wrongdoers, as if the old order could be restored, such a restorative interpretation does violence to the text and the course of action. No, Shakespeare takes the liberty of depicting a downfall without resurrection, the family conflicts without resolution, the all-too-human burden of development without redemption. In this way, the reader or viewer is unchecked by the force of negativity. Such empty spaces and negations, however, "initiate an interaction in the course of which the contours of what has been left empty are occupied by the reader's ideas" (Iser, 1980, p. 144). The reader or viewer is called upon to realise the threefold negativity:

first, of human life leading to old age and death; second, of the family rifts based on untriangulated relationships; and third, of the unresolved social contradictions and ruptures. The reader or spectator will have to deal with these negatives, hopefully in a different way compared to the protagonists of the play.

I want to return to my central question concerning the potential for hope. Where does the reader or spectator find a perspective to address the future in view of a piece that is "more of a wound than the critical tradition has cared to acknowledge" (Bloom, 1998, p. 491)? Even if the play shows us that all human beings are fools, as a disguise or as a protection or as a sign of despair, it shows something else at the same time:

> Shakespeare lavishes his own genius, at its most exuberant, upon Lear's greatness, a splendor surpassing that of the biblical Solomon's. Lear's utterances establish a standard of measurement that no other fictive personae can approach, the limits of human capacity for profoundly affect are consistently transcended by Lear.
>
> (Bloom, 1998, p. 491)

It is worth taking Harold Bloom's unjust, polemical, clever, and passionate partisanship of Shakespeare seriously. The language in which the play is written is so vivid, so charged with emotions, and very innovative, adding over a hundred words to the English language (Wells, 2000, p. 53). Moreover, it is located at the limits of linguistic expression. Language reaches its limits in *King Lear*, or rather, the play is a passionate attempt to explore and expand the possibilities of language.

"Speak what we feel, not what we ought to say" (24.319)—to once again bring the concluding, penultimate phrase of the play to mind, placed in the mouth of Albany's inconspicuous figure. Hope lies where language expands man's knowledge of himself and his own affects. It is not without reason that the jester is one of the decisive figures in the drama. He cannot change the world he experiences—he does not intervene in the course of events, but he remains at Lear's side and, with his linguistic wit, he demonstrates, at the limits of comprehensibility, what language is capable of, but also where its limits lie.

On the chances and dead-ends of saying "no"—*Bartleby the Scrivener* (H. Melville)

D ealing with negative symptoms is and remains a major challenge for clinical therapeutic practice. Is mutism—the denial
of communication or food—an expression of a loss of abilities,
or does an understanding approach to such behavioural patterns possibly enable one to find meaning in them? In this chapter, I will not
present any patients or case reports; instead, I use a text that allows us
to ask this question in a new way, even if the text itself is not new at all,
rather, more than 150 years old. Herman Melville's narrative *Bartleby
the Scrivener* deals with negativity in a way that was completely unusual
for his time; he was ahead of his time, and it is precisely for this reason
that it has sparked a discussion that is still alive and productive today.

This fascination needs to be understood. I will show that negativity,
negation, to say "no", to withdraw, to reject, in whatever form negativity may be realised, must always be linked to the other. That it is
fatal when the "no", which is always the negation of something, of a
statement of an other, is attributed to the individual person only, as his
or her feature—as his or her trait or deficit. But what the "no" has to
say to the other remains open; whether it is a "no" by which someone
destroys themselves, the other, or the contact between them, or whether

the "no" entails a self-preservation, even self-assertion, as well, that is to be examined in each case.

Bartleby: text and text reception

The text

In 1851, Herman Melville publishes his great novel *Moby-Dick*, which initially does not see much success. One year later, his next novel, *Pierre*, is published, which seems to be a complete failure. Melville has monetary troubles, he has to feed a family with three children. He agrees to publish stories in a magazine on a regular basis to earn money. The first story, published in the November and December editions of *Harper's New Monthly Magazine* in 1853, is the story of a writer, but one who only copies.

The story is told quickly: Bartleby is hired as a law copyist—a clerk—in a law firm. He is the fourth clerk in the office, as the first-person narrator, the lawyer, reports. The workplace is cramped, and Bartleby is assigned an office that does not allow a view outside, because walls everywhere obstruct the view. The fact that the place of action is New York, an illustrious address, fits in well with this. Wall Street—the reader is indeed introduced to a wall street, there are walls everywhere, inside and outside, because even in the office, the view is obstructed by screens.

On the third day, Bartleby utters his famous formula for the first time: "I prefer not to." He prefers not to heed a request for stooge services from the boss and not to leave his niche. Next, he does not want to participate in reviewing the copies, that is, he prefers not to do so, and in fact he is exempted from this obligation. Soon he will also give up copying. But on the other hand, he does not want to be dismissed either. He does not leave the firm, even when asked to do so. He does not leave it at all, and soon he will just stand rigidly in the room and refuse all requests. The lawyer is finally forced to move out of his own office; if Bartleby does not leave, he himself is forced to leave to get rid of him. But even moving out does not help, as the landlord of the Wall Street flat comes forward and reports that Bartleby simply remains in the apartment and must be removed. The lawyer again tries to persuade him, tries to remove him—all in vain. Finally, Bartleby is disposed of with police power into the prison, "Tombs". From there, the lawyer is called again, because nobody is able to figure out what Bartleby means to say, and he will not eat anything. Finally, he ceases to move anymore, which the lawyer experiences during his last visit—and his death shortly thereafter is not even included in the plot, but is only added as an afterthought.

But the story is not that short, after all, the Penguin paperback edition has forty-five pages. There is hardly anything to say about Bartleby, since he always does the same thing, namely, to refuse to act. All the more, the lawyer tells the reader about his own emotional states, about the wide range of feelings he experiences, about the anger, but also about the strange closeness that he feels to Bartleby. There is almost no information about Bartleby; the contours he gains are derived from his emotional life and from the lawyer's reactions described above.

Only at the very end does the first-person narrator mention, if not a biographical fact, then at least a rumour: Bartleby used to work in an office, a branch of the post office, so to speak, that was responsible for processing letters that did not arrive at their destination. These undeliverable letters are called "dead letters" in the English text. The story ends in a strange turn: "On errands of life, these letters speed to death. O Bartleby, o humanity!" The paradoxical juxtaposition of death and life is noticeable in the phrase: the letters are messages of life, and it is precisely on this path that they rush towards death.

The text has been translated into many languages, and some translations don't preserve this tension between life and death. Take the German translation as an example: "Auf den Irrungen des Lebens treiben diese Briefe dem Tode zu. O Bartleby! O Menschlichkeit." The phrase can be translated backwards as: "On the trials and tribulations of life, these letters drift towards death." Thus, the enormous tension built up within a single sentence is considerably downplayed. It is also interesting that there is an intertextual reference that the Italian philosopher Agamben (1991, p. 269) has discovered, to a letter of Paul to the Romans from the Bible (Romans 7.10). The decisive passage in the English translation that Melville had in hand was: "And the commandment which was ordained to life I found to be unto death." This text is obviously about life and death, and beyond that about the entanglement of life with death, about the fact that that which serves life carries death within itself.

The reception

Psychopathological and psychoanalytical reception

Pathologising Bartleby makes for a superficial reading. Bartleby personifies negativism in the context of a psychotic event, where the retreat to saying "no" expands to an increasingly radical defence against contact, evolving from the rejection of language and the refusal of food to immobility and death, which are symptoms of catatonic psychosis: "This form of fear and avoidance of reality (sc. of the psychotic) is perhaps most impressively portrayed in literary terms in the short story *Bartleby* by Herman Melville", the Swiss psychiatrist Daniel Hell (2003, p. 169) formulates. Even psychoanalytic discourse is not free of the pathologising attitude, for example, when Bartleby is accused of arrogant narcissism and an attitude of disguised omnipotence (Asch, 1976), or when a syndrome of apathy is explained by using or misusing Bartleby as an example (Peniazek, 1982). Finally, the prototype of the melancholic in psychodynamic terms is apparent in Bartleby (Hassoun, 1995).

These forms of text reception are revealing, certainly not for the text, but for the relationship between psychopathology and literature. For it is obvious that the psychopathologising interpretation reaches through the text, as it were, and detaches the figure of Bartleby from his surroundings, from the relationships that surround him, and from the literary form that generates him. Literature then remains an arsenal for interesting casuistry. The encounter between literature and psychopathology shows exhaustive examples—neither is the reading of literature extended by psychopathology, nor does literature extend psychiatry. Let us consider that a diagnostic attitude applied to literature interpretation is not productive, but it isn't sufficient either in a clinical perspective, though it still can be found in psychiatric diagnostics, in the sense of the medical-psychiatric view which aims at identifying a symptom by "looking through" a patient (Foucault, 1973) and ignoring his personality. If biography or the history of relational interactions is left out, the ensuing reductionism is very inadequate. This holds true in therapeutic practice as well as in the interpretation of literature.

Some analytical works on *Bartleby* did not get stuck in the diagnostic attitude, but rather they focused on the relationship between the lawyer and Bartleby. They see Bartleby as the lawyer's projection, and this is precisely what explains the uncanny feeling that surrounds the story: Bartleby is, in a way, a double of the lawyer, and as such, he seems to be an uncanny person (Feigelson, 1993). This is an interesting thought, which will be taken up anew in the conclusion I will draw in the end. This interpretation, which puts the lawyer and his projections in the foreground, is not very far from another, initially surprising one, which compares the sensory shield surrounding Bartleby's office—then, open to mutual projections—with the seclusion the classical psychoanalytical situation allows, the couch being in the centre (Levy & Inderbitzin, 1989).

Because they take what happens in the relationship into account, these latter interpretations go further than the psychopathologically reductive ones that were mentioned at the beginning. And yet they remain merely applicative interpretations: psychoanalytic experiences are retrieved in the text; whereas this may be important for the confirmation of psychoanalytic experience, it does not go much further than that. It may be useful to shed some light on the mystery of the encounter described in the text through paralleling psychoanalytic events and literary relations—more cannot be gained in this way. One could also judge more negatively, vary the end of *Bartleby*, and say: "On errands of life, these interpretations speed to death", meaning that such interpretations, while intending to communicate new insights, are, in a way, dead-end streets.

A philosophical reception

How would one read the text in a non-reductive way? The philosopher G. Deleuze (1997) has dealt with Bartleby and his formula in a small book. Deleuze is an attentive reader, with a free-floating attention and accuracy in his reading that an analyst could not improve upon in his practice. Deleuze also reads without reservation and does not deny that the main figure, Bartleby, is characterised by psychotic experiences. But this insight does not prevent him from reading without blinkers, and in the process, he brings out important layers of the text:

1. When does Bartleby use the formula "I prefer not to"? Deleuze highlights all the passages one by one, and by describing them neatly, he slowly unveils the effect of the formula. It does not serve to explain already existing attitudes, but rather creates new behaviours and new

conditions in dealing with each other: the refusal to communicate by talking is the beginning, and consequences follow. This is the performative power of the formula. By the way, the formula is contagious, evidenced by the fact that it is used more and more often by the others, which has a strange but also uncanny effect.

2. What distinguishes the formula? It is negative, it is against an expectation, but Bartleby does not simply say "no". The formula does not negate a specific object; Bartleby only speaks of himself, that he prefers not to do this or that. He postpones the consequences. Deleuze reads the text literally: Bartleby, the lawyer says in the text, is a writer without references, that is, a job applicant without a recommendation. Deleuze recognises that the lack of references is actually a fitting characterisation of Bartleby—that the formula constitutes a language without reference. It dissolves the reference to an object, but also the reference of the self to the other, which is contained in the ordinary speech act. Thus, the formula drives everyone to madness, because it is directed against the self-definitions implied in a concrete speech act. Bartleby's formula is directed against the common and recognised language games; so it is only consequent that he refuses to reproduce words in his job as a copyist. But this is precisely what his effect is based on; his colleagues might be original and witty, but of Turkey, Nippers, and Ginger Nut nothing much remains because they play along with the language game, while Bartleby dissolves it. The formula heralds that a completely different linguistic order might be possible by creating a "zone of indistinctness, indistinguishability", a "glide", an "absolute contiguity" (1997, p. 31).

3. What kind of negativity is brought forward in *Bartleby*? Deleuze does not understand Bartleby's non-actions as a will to nothing, but rather, as the abandonment of will, that is, a nothingness of will that manifests itself precisely in this indeterminacy. Bartleby is put into context with a number of other figures invented by Melville and other nineteenth-century literature. Deleuze takes up a term used elsewhere by Melville, that of "the original", to characterise Bartleby and several other figures. Originals are beings of the so-called "first nature", a nature prior to socialisation, and they are contrasted by the lawyers or, generally speaking, the people of the "second nature", who are on the side of the law and our normal life. Originals then are

the "demons" who deconstruct the law and bring down the paternal order, to use a Lacanian phrase. The world is unmasked as a masquerade, without a new world being constituted in its place.

4. How is the text situated historically and politically? Not for nothing, Deleuze believes, the text was created in the nineteenth-century USA. According to its founding history, America is understood as a protest against the English father generation, as an uprising against fathers, as an attempt to establish a society of brothers. With *Bartleby*, Melville illustrated the failure not only of the lawyer, but of America's founding idea altogether. Thus, the end becomes more understandable: "Schizophrenic vocation: even as a catatonic and anorexic, Bartleby is not the sick person, but the doctor of a sick America, the Medicine Man, the new Christ or brother of us all" (p. 60).

Why this detailed presentation? Deleuze is not a psychoanalyst—rather, he criticises psychoanalysis for its historical blindness (p. 56). And yet, as mentioned at the beginning, his method is related to the method of the analyst, who remains openly attentive to what he encounters. The method can be characterised by what it declines to do: it does not pathologise, it does not allow itself to be seduced into making false declarations by reducing the event to a psychopathological template. It also does not—at least not at first—interpret deep into the text, but takes it seriously and literally. It pays particular attention to language and the forms of relationships that are created through speaking or by the refusal of articulated language, that is, by speaking differently. The diagnostic question, centred around Bartleby's madness revealing itself by repeating his formula ever so often, blinds us to the subtle description of language effects.

It is interesting now to see that Deleuze does not stop at the analysis of negative communication. He sees in Bartleby not only the one who blows up communication guidelines, but also a prophet and healer. But what constitutes his prophecies is not written in Melville's literary work. Deleuze implements into the text his own concern to break up the father-determined social order and create a fraternal coexistence. In the end, the negativity of the text reverses into the positivity of a statement—the patient becoming the doctor. It seems as if it was infinitely difficult, perhaps too difficult, for Deleuze to remain in a state of indecision.

Resistance in the text

Why does a text tempt one to write more and more about it? What is unexploited about it is the very fact that it is irritating, that it cannot be brought to a point; the text does not suggest a false conclusiveness, but points to the incompleteness of the symbolising processes, the incompleteness of the symbolic, dealing with it both in terms of content and form. We have seen that this incompleteness is a provocation both for the protagonists in the text and the interpreters reading the text. The struggle for closure becomes concretely visible in the narrative through the description of the Wall Street office walls. It is also evident in the relationships between Bartleby and the other protagonists, in their constant attempt to incorporate, capture, and fixate the enigmatic Bartleby, but it is precisely through this that Bartleby insists all the more on his enigmatic nature. (He behaves like the unconscious signifier brought forward by Jacques Lacan.) The struggle for closure is reproduced in the interpretations of the text that try to pocket him psychopathologically, that lock him up in a clinical prison, as it were. It also manifests itself in a sort of text defusion by downgrading it to the mere place of theory application. And finally, it reveals itself in a subtle way in abrupt positivisation, which turns out to be a projective or usurpatory handling of the text as well, in that its blanks are used as a projection screen for the contents of one's own imagination, theories, and concepts.

Bartleby is a law copyist who refuses to reproduce laws. Any interpretation of the text runs the risk of becoming a copied, reproduced law. Thus one can also understand the text as a critique of interpretation. A psychoanalytical "art of interpretation" (Loch, 1993) would have to learn from the text and, first of all, from its interpretations. Processes of closure are forms of reaction aimed at dealing with negativity. To recognise, avoid, and dissolve them would be the task of psychoanalytic interpretation in clinical work:

1. What is not understood does not need to be interpreted immediately, but rather can be enriched by associations and intertextual

references (on the part of the analyst, on the part of the analysand). Thus, enrichment takes the place of explanation.

2. Usurpation, occupation of what appears as a void and as such creates a horror vacui, seems inevitable. Psychoanalysis is privileged (and only so credible) in that it reflects steps of therapeutic usurpation critically aiming at reversing it, for example in the analysis of countertransference.

3. Every negativity tends to be positivised, and it always remains to be checked whether it does not have to defend itself against such positivation again.

In other words, a psychoanalysis that applies its schemes like any other psychopathology, that does not worry about the literal, that is on the side of the world's lawyers and law and order, does not deserve to be taken seriously as an independent science.

Psychoanalysis and the therapeutic work on and with negativity

What follows now are some variations on the final sentence of the narrative, which has already been quoted several times, and which seems to me to be, if not the key, then at least the pivotal point of the narrative. I will proceed on two levels, first on the level of text content, then on the level of text reception, and simultaneously on the level of literary self-reflection. I will thus first deal with Bartleby as a pseudo-person, as if he were a human being, in order to then turn to the question of what fascinates us about the text. Closely related to this is the question of what statements the text makes about literature and, beyond that, about writing and speaking itself.

Content

Does the literary person Bartleby have a message? If he has one, it is dead, dead letter, undeliverable. It does not reach its addressee. And yet it is a message of life—an errand in the service of life. The subject is not switched off, rather it expresses itself by preferring, by giving preference to something, but what it prefers remains in negation. In negation, one can hear the messages of life only negatively.

What can psychoanalysis contribute to understanding the life-related message of "no"? Let us begin, as always, with Freud and his significant work on negation from 1925 (1925h, pp. 235–239), in which Freud highlighted two positive aspects of negation. The first is that denial allows the consciousness to take note of an idea, even if its emotional meaning remains denied ("I didn't mean to hurt you", except that I unconsciously wished to do so). The second is that denial, and therefore negation as well, is connected to the differentiation of inside and outside: what is denied is originally attributed to the outside world. That which is not good is seen as coming from outside: "You are evil; I am very good."

Psychoanalytic object relations theory according to Freud understood the step of drawing the boundary between inside and outside as the boundary between self and other. If a developmentally adequate demarcation from the one who becomes an object through this demarcation is not possible, for example, because there has been no affective resonance from the beginning, because the primary caregiver wraps up the emerging child self in his or her own needs in such a way that distancing is not possible, the child remains always a "cork child" (McDougall, 1989, p. 78), part of the mother's self, and so on. What is then left to work on? A desperate form of demarcation, of negation work—"travail du négatif", as André Green (1993) calls it—is to create an emptiness through the destruction of perception, be it reality, be it one's own feelings, that is a substitute for an adequate distance from the other. The prototype of negation work is the negative hallucination, the hallucination of emptiness, a nothingness that ranges from the destruction of a perception (as in the dreams of the "Wolf Man") to the extinction of affects in psychosomatic sufferings, and finally to a "délir de négation", the nihilistic delusion in which, as it were, nothing exists anymore.

This self-created understanding of emptiness is clinically extremely consequential as an attempt to distance oneself, in which intrusions or separations become so complete that the formation of representations in an "aerated space" between self and object is not possible. In Winnicott's terms, one can understand negativity as an attempt to create potential spaces—spaces of possibility. Deficiency cannot simply be described as the failure of an ego performance, as a defect, but rather as an attempt—however unfavourable and disadvantageous—to protect oneself through the negation (of feeling, perception, thinking).

This is an extremely important position for clinical practice. I will leave Bartleby for a moment and give some clinical examples:

1. Is the return of the trauma, the self-dramatised re-enactment of the unbearable in (delicate or pronounced) self-harm, not an attempt to preserve one's own subjectivity? Just as Bartleby's use of "I prefer not to" rescues subjectivity against all objects that have become indifferent, so the self-induced repetition of the trauma is also an attempt to experience oneself. When one's own horizon is filled with pain, it is easier to inflict pain on one's own body, and thus experience a minimal self-efficacy, than to passively let oneself be bent by the pain.

2. Is the destruction of communication in the psychotic residual state—the destruction of the relationship by complete withdrawal—an attempt to create an interior space where there previously was none, that is, to defend oneself against constantly repeated intrusive experiences by creating a void?

3. Is the anorexic self-starvation of an adolescent who may die of self-destruction also an attempt to save the parents who, without having to care for a sick child—and without a child at all—would be forced to face their own unfulfilled lives? Does the child sacrifice herself to save the parents and remain both sick and a child?

4. Is the suicidal act, even as a completed suicide, also an—albeit desperate—statement? Does it hold true when someone suddenly, seemingly without motivation, departs from life in a way that may be regarded as completely inappropriate to her previous lifestyle or her value system? The person who fell victim to a suicide might have seemed psychologically healthy before; often, they will be regarded as mentally ill for the first time post-mortem. But this does not help; it would be much more appropriate to listen to and understand the suicidal act as an action statement, as it were, a form of staging one's innermost feelings, representations, and thoughts which never had a place in relationships and find representation only in the suicide itself.

Seen in this light, the story *Bartleby the Scrivener* reads like the report on a person who constantly strives to draw a line to delimit himself. The problems of demarcation are presented in a very concrete and pervasive manner. Bartleby gets light through a window, but he has no view outside because the window is blocked by the attached houses. He also has no view to the inside, because the lawyer puts up a green folding screen, which obstructs eye contact, but does not shield it acoustically. It is a cocoon, like a womb, in which Bartleby is enclosed. No wonder the lawyer finds him in a foetal position when paying a visit in prison ("Tombs"): "Strangely huddled at the base of the wall, his knees drawn up, and lying on his side, his head touching the cold stones" (1985, p. 99). Bartleby lives in the office and cannot be removed from it—only by force. He no longer acts according to his duties because he does not tolerate the socially coded definitions of relationships. He feeds himself less and less because he does not want to be fed from outside. Obviously, Bartleby urgently needs the demarcation, but his negation does not succeed to install it. His formula has a purpose in life, but it has the opposite effect, it only accelerates death.

When we talk about the messages of life, there must not only be a sender, but also a receiver. There must be a willingness to engage with the narrative. It depends not only on the individual pathology—the indissoluble ambivalence—and not only on the ability to convey a message, but also to listen to it. In the 1970s, the great philosopher Klaus Heinrich (1978) wrote a book with the meaningful title *Versuch über die Schwierigkeit Nein zu sagen* (translation: Attempt on the difficulty of saying no), a philosophical work dedicated to the forms of contradiction, objection, and thus also commitment. "Bartleby" stands for the complementary difficulty of taking "no" seriously, of hearing "no" at all, it stands for the challenge of working on the limits of comprehensibility and meaning, and also of asking about a person's activity in preserving his subjectivity even in the destruction of meaning. It is precisely because of the irritation and provocation that this entails that the text is important for our clinical work. In any case, the challenge of asking for the meaning of the negative, the silencing, the emptiness, is always an important driving force behind the work of psychoanalysts in psychiatry.

Reception

Why are we fascinated by such a text? Why has it been received for over 150 years, why is it still being worked on? Why do we read it today? In other words: does the writer Melville have a message that he wants to convey with this text? Is this message also dead—a non-deliverable dead letter? Or does it reach its addressee?

The thoughts that now follow completely de-pathologise Bartleby; they make him a figure who is—or was—familiar to us in our own life history. Let us not forget: Bartleby is not a patient or a human being, but a literary figure. And the author demonstrates to us that language is not capable of creating order, even if it is always used anew for this purpose. At the same time, the distancing function of language fails; speaking does not enable Bartleby to separate himself from the lawyer. It is as if Melville is constantly re-examining the point at which language works on separation. It is as if he is holding on to an essential point in a struggle for separation that is somehow familiar to all of us and that is connected to the beginning of language development. It is a fight between life and death that leads to the demarcation of the self—to individuation.

Julia Kristeva, the semiotician and psychoanalyst, has devoted much of her professional life to exploring the connections between the development of language and of relational bonds. How does the symbolic order form, what precedes it? This is the crucial question for Kristeva. She connects developmental stages with linguistic competence; she assigns to the stage where the motherly object and the child are still not separated a layer of communication which she calls "the semiotic" and in which linguistic signs are still effective through their materiality, their tone, their rhythmicity, and the affects resonating within them. The semiotic is contrasted with "the symbolic" as it describes a developed, content-related, grammatical language function. What interests her is not so much the steps in the development from the semiotic to the symbolic, but rather the interweaving of the two levels of signs in literary texts. The symbolic does not overcome the semiotic but remains related to it.

Let's formulate the relationships in a developmental psychological way for a while longer. It is the demarcation from the matrix, the maternal tissue, the chora, which is necessary but never fully succeeds. To attain the level of the symbolic order is, at the same time and concomitant with all the gains, connected with a loss. What is lost appears at first in a kind of proto- or archaic symbolisation, without ever being able to be properly grasped symbolically. What the matrix had been in a pre-symbolic time is now experienced as devouring, threatening, and persecuting. Following in Freud's footsteps, Kristeva investigates how the self constitutes itself by forming representations that now allow it to distance itself from the maternal chora—in this way, the so-called abjects are created, even before the objects. The abject—the horrible, disgusting, incomprehensible—forms itself as something that is differentiated from the self but does not yet have clear contours and is the first product from which the emerging self must separate.

The theory of the abject radicalises Freud's concept of negation by attempting to capture the experiential quality of the very first developmental steps toward a symbolised experience of the world, and in doing so emphasises the experiences of demarcation, cutting off, and exclusion that accompany the symbolisation steps. Feelings of dread, horror, disgust, and so on are the emotional sides of this loss. The abject precedes the symbolic differentiation and prepares for it. The abject remains threateningly uncanny, because it does not respect boundaries, and it remains present in experiences of decay and disgust. "We may call it a border; abjection is above all ambiguity. Because, while releasing a hold, it does not radically cut off the subject from what threatens it—on the contrary, abjection acknowledges it to be in perpetual danger" (Kristeva, 1980, p. 9). Abjects can be found everywhere as the excluded and the rejected, in the individual imagination as well as in religions, world views, works of art, and in literary texts. Where the symbolic orders cast a doubt on themselves as to their binding capacities and try to become aware of their preconditions, abjective experiences are significant. Probably the clearest presentation and most reflected criticism of the concept of abjection is given by Winfried Menninghaus (1999, 2003).

Kristeva locates the aesthetic experience by repeatedly tracking down the fragile boundaries of language to its speechless origin (p. 13); this characterisation is precisely true of Melville's text. Let us not forget: the text is written from the perspective of the lawyer. This lawyer moves on the safe ground of his legal system and his language order. Actually, his—and not so much Bartleby's—behaviour needs explanation; what is surprising is the fact that he cannot really distance himself from Bartleby, indeed, that in the end, when he visits Bartleby in prison, he calls him his friend. We can see Bartleby as the lawyer's abject, as the one the lawyer has given up in order to adapt to his world, which incidentally—in an all-too-familiar image—is in the shadow of Wall

Street, and thus by no means autonomous or self-sufficient. Bartleby is the necessarily discarded flip side of this order, which always shines through, and from which we cannot separate ourselves when we speak.

Through the concept of abjection, some important passages of *Bartleby*'s text, which have already been dealt with, are now understandable in a new way. The emphasis of the closing phrase "O Bartleby! O humanity!" becomes more understandable in its ambiguity. It not only appeals to the compassion, that is, the humanity of the reader, in the face of such a fate, but at the same time addresses every human being. This exclamation, at the latest, calls for a transference of what the lawyer as representative of human experience has already felt in the text to the reader: they can rediscover themselves in Bartleby. Thus, Bartleby does not embody the insane person—the psychotic—the one who struggles through negation and rejection for demarcation and his own sphere of experience. Bartleby also refers to a position in human development, namely the original demarcation in self-development, as if the text were to record a transitory position in human experience, just as a film can be stopped in its course—a position of transition that is never completely overcome throughout life. Rather, the text appeals to us as readers because the process of symbolisation and the losses enforced by it remain virulent as threads at all times. From here, the formula, "On errands of life, the letters speed to death", which immediately precedes the final turn, reveals a deeper meaning. "Letters" are not only the posted letters, but also the letters of the alphabet—the basic building blocks of the symbolic. They transport the messages of life, but they also refer to the experience of death inherent in the process of symbolisation.

Since literature is inevitably and necessarily anchored in the symbolic, it does not find it easy to capture such experiences at the limits of the symbolic. The formula "I prefer not to ..." creates a sounding space that fulfils a semiotic function. It cannot be reduced to a common denominator, but is "contagious", and this effect, a sort of repetition compulsion inherent in a formula that can never be mastered by assigning a final meaning, is demonstrated in the text itself. Moreover, every work that continues to deal with the narrative, including this one, bears witness to this fascination. Even the concluding phrase, which has already been quoted several times above, is located at the limits of meaning: "On errands of life, these letters speed to death", a second formula and a very lyrical one indeed, which sticks in one's mind without ever losing its ambiguity, its disseminative function.

On the other hand, Melville's narrative retains a traditional form. In the history of literature, it must be situated at the beginning of a tendency both in literature and the visual arts to gauge the limits of the symbolic, the limits of giving meaning through language and art—a tendency that later on became dominant in the twentieth century. Because this paradox of using language to characterise its very limits has not yet become one-sided in Melville's work, it is and remains attractive and effective. It is as if the text involves the reader in the dynamics of the disruption of a symbolic order as one intersubjectively shared. It deals with the dangers that emanate from the one who negates or must negate it, and that affect those who cling to it, but for whom it has become fragile. Thus, it is consistent that Melville lets us experience Bartleby from the perspective of the lawyer, who is a man of law and symbolic order. The text has not left the symbolic order behind, but it does not merely play with it, it allows its cracks to be experienced without already representing an afterlife—the semiotic becomes palpable, but not easily grasped. Precisely because of this, it remains more eerie than in those later texts that want to represent the semiotic in itself, that turn their backs on the symbolic, but perhaps precisely because of this defuse the described field of tension.

Outlook

Bartleby has siblings. The fact that the text insists and remains a provocation has led not only to attempts at scientific interpretation, but also to literary imitations. A Spanish author, E. Vila-Matas (2001), has humorously and fictiously worked out the intertextuality in which Bartleby finds himself, using literary means. He inquires into the work of authors who no longer write, who have refused to speak—the Bartlebys in literature (Borens, 2001). The result is nevertheless a book that has actually been written. To depict the loss of language in language is necessarily a paradox. And yet it is not a whimsical idea, but the paradox of language itself.

Bartleby—or should I say Melville?—has siblings not only in literature, but also in philosophy. The Italian philosopher Agamben, who has been cited above, sees a kinship of Bartleby to the philosophers of scepticism who have highlighted the state of suspense, the state of mere possibility, the "ou mallon" in ancient Greek. This is the difficult alternative—the uncertain chance; in this context, Agamben emphasises the pure potentiality that Bartleby's formula makes possible. But the possibilities it contains are the unexhausted chances of the past. This makes sense: the dead letters are testimonies of the past that have no addressee in the present. Bartleby thus becomes a relative of Walter Benjamin, whose philosophy of history was essentially concerned with the unexhausted, outstanding claims of the past.

But let's be careful not to trivialise the text again by forgetting that the letters' message just doesn't get through. More than twenty years ago, Ludger Lütkehaus (1999) wrote a book with the simple title *Nichts* (Nothing), in which he emphasised nihilophobia—the inability to think of nothing. The Nothing is deified in mysticism, it is dialectically seen as creative in philosophy, which turns the nothingness into the lightening Nothing. It is difficult to prefer the "not to"; Bartleby—or Melville— would have felt understood by Lütkehaus.

Bartleby insists. As a psychoanalyst, I can not only interpret a text, but conversely, I am also interpreted by it or disturbed in my interpretations. I can't contribute a decisive, all-dissolving interpretation. Bartleby insists: the meaning of the text is still missing. Effective literature does not dissolve into a factual text through understanding. The decisive question now is whether the same applies to the therapeutic sciences of the psyche: do they leave room for the heterogeneous that cannot be incorporated? Does the sting of the foreign, of the other or the alien, remain a challenge for an understanding that nevertheless avoids totalisation? Otherwise, psychiatrists and psychotherapists will become the advocates of reason, close to Wall Street, big money and walls in their minds. The humanity that the text invokes with its last word can be measured precisely by this question, whether Bartleby is silenced in one way or another, or whether his "I prefer not to ..." remains a provocation.

CHAPTER 3

Aesthetic form and unconscious sense: self-care and identity in *Moby-Dick* (H. Melville)

From its very beginning, psychoanalysis has dealt not only with clinical cases but also with works of the visual arts and of literature as objects of psychoanalytic research. Freud repeatedly discussed the essential motivations for psychoanalysis to deal with poets or literary texts or with artists and works of art. First and foremost, psychoanalysis can provide in-depth biographical research of the author.

> When psychoanalysis puts itself at the service of biography, it naturally has the right to be treated no more harshly than the latter itself. Psychoanalysis can supply some information which cannot be arrived at by other means and can thus demonstrate new connecting threads in the "weaver's masterpiece" spread between the instinctual endowments, the experiences and the works of an artist.
>
> (Freud, 1930d, p. 212)

Psychoanalytic interpretation of the author has to defend itself against the accusation of reductionism.

> When psychiatric research, normally content to draw on frailer men for its material, approaches one who is among the greatest of the human race, it is not doing so for the reasons so frequently ascribed to it by laymen. "To blacken the radiant and drag the sublime into the dust" is no part of its purpose, and there is no satisfaction for it in narrowing the gulf which separates the perfection of the great from the inadequacy of the objects that are its usual concern.
>
> (Freud, 1910c, p. 63)

With these words, Freud immediately justifies his preoccupation with Leonardo da Vinci. This justification no longer seems necessary to us today, since we no longer have any interest in elevating our poets to Olympus. Nevertheless, there is a variety of reductionism that has remained relevant throughout the history of psychoanalytical literary interpretation, namely, the reduction of a work's content to the psychodynamics of the author. If the work is read only from the point of view of the hidden references it contains to the author's psychopathology, the work itself is lost from view.

A further contribution that psychoanalysis can make to literary analysis lies in extending models of aesthetic reception by taking unconscious processes into account. In this context, reading was conceived as a process of countertransference. This aspect, too, is already pre-formulated in Freud's work:

> We laymen have always been intensely curious to know—like the Cardinal who put a similar question to Ariosto—from what sources that strange being, the creative writer, draws his material, and how he manages to make such an impression on us with it and to arouse in us emotions of which, perhaps, we had not even thought ourselves capable.
>
> (Freud, 1908e, p. 143)

Psychoanalysis contributes not only to the understanding of author and reader, but also to the understanding of literary figures. They can be analysed just as persons can be analysed; conversely, new psychological insights can be gained from literary texts. Thus, psychoanalysis can be oriented to human fate, "which great writers have created from the wealth of their knowledge of the mind" (Freud, 1916d, p. 318).

However enriching psychoanalytic concepts may be for the psychological study of a literary or art work, they always remain subject to the reproach of ignoring or even levelling out what makes the work of art a work of art in the first place, namely its aesthetic form. The heroes of a novel or a play can quickly become cases, as can their authors, and at the end of some psychoanalytic literary interpretation, the reader may wonder whether he or she could not have learned more from a clinical case history than from the often clinically distorted view of a work of art. Neglect of the aesthetic form in literary interpretation has a further consequence: the relationship between psychoanalysis and literature becomes one-sided, the literary work becomes an application, an object—arbitrarily interchangeable in principle—on which psychoanalytic constructs are tried out or to which they are applied. In this way, however, psychoanalytic interpretation closes itself off from the possibilities of learning from the work of art or from theories of art, and it becomes tautological. The subsequent attempt to psychoanalytically re-read Herman Melville's novel *Moby-Dick* attempts to avoid these reductionist pitfalls.

A brief look at the author

Herman Melville was born in 1819 as the third child of Allan and Maria Melvill (at that time written without the final e). Due to the sudden death of his father when Herman was twelve, the family as a safe place collapsed, and the son was forced to pursue various breadwinning occupations without being able to find a permanent occupation. At the age of nineteen, he eventually found a job as a sailor and went to sea on various voyages. At twenty-one, he joined a whaling expedition, left the ship en route, signed on to another boat, and survived numerous adventures. They became the subject of his first novels. Only at the age of twenty-four did he return home, and he worked as a writer, with varying success. He married Elisabeth and tried to earn money for the family as a professional writer.

In 1850, he met Nathaniel Hawthorne, with whom he became close friends; the author of the book *The Scarlet Letter* had already made a name for himself by then. Under Hawthorne's influence, *Moby-Dick* was written in 1851. Like the other books, *Moby-Dick* was received with varying degrees of benevolence by critics. Melville's writing career was endangered. He continued to write, but could no longer support his family, so he ultimately became a customs inspector in the Port of New York. This failure must have been very hard on him, and it was experienced as a heavy burden by his family. Nevertheless, his literary productivity remained somewhat unbroken, and one of Melville's most important stories, *Bartleby the Scrivener*, was written during this time. The work *Billy Budd* was not published during his lifetime, but later consolidated Melville's fame, not least through the opera version by Benjamin Britten. Melville died in 1891.

Psychoanalytic reception of Melville

Since Melville has gone down in literary history as one of the most important American authors of the nineteenth century, it is not surprising that psychoanalytic authors have frequently dealt with Melville, especially in the USA. Their approaches to Melville's oeuvre fit neatly in the different categories of psychoanalytic literary interpretation summarised in the introduction. Either the author is analysed through his literary texts, or the texts are related to life history data, or the characters of the novels are analysed as if they were real human beings. From a psychoanalytic historical perspective, it is interesting to see how, for the time being, the prevailing theoretical debate within psychoanalysis is reflected in the interpretative patterns of the novels.

Over the years, Melville's person has been viewed from many different angles. Weaver (1921) is probably the first to examine the mother–son relationship. The mother is described as an energetic but tough woman who is said to have had a remarkable ability to have angry outbursts. The son is described as being similar to her. They are said to have had a kind of love–hate relationship (see also Miller, 1975).

Others emphasise the father–son relationship; this topic is obvious because of the father's manic-depressive illness and his early death. Chase (1949) emphasises that Melville had a crucial need to split up his father's image, as it were, in order to maintain an acceptable image of the father in relation to the father dying in mania. The monograph by Tolchin (1988) examines Melville's life documents and adopts the perspective of suppressed grief or unsuccessful mourning. It examines the relationship with the mother in terms of how she fostered the lifelong inability to mourn the father's early death. The study is interesting because the psychodynamic theories on Melville's unfinished mourning and the literature interpretation that follows are related to the social coding of mourning processes in the nineteenth century. Melville's examination of the social norms of Victorian-influenced America thus creates an intersection between poetry, the person, and social history. Tolchin interprets the novel *Moby-Dick* in such a way that one of the novel's main heroes, Ahab, represents a literary externalisation of a father imago; Ahab's monomania reflects manic episodes shortly before the death of the father. Psychoanalytically, however, the portrayal is made more complex by the fact that it is not the inner image that the son has of the father, but rather, what he takes over from the mother, since the mother does not conclude her mourning process. From this perspective, *Moby-Dick* would be an attempt to perform mourning work after all— to detach from the persecuting inner object of the father, to depict it, but also to transform it into a tragic and ultimately heroic figure.

In later psychoanalytic publications on Melville, the unsuccessful mourning work continues to play a decisive role. Boker (1996) combines a feminist reading of American literature with the psychoanalytic perspective of imperfect mourning. The interesting new aspect of this interpretation is that the difficulties of mourning are disguised against the background of American masculine socialisation. This perspective allows a new reading of *Moby-Dick*. The fact that this novel is primarily a men's novel appears in a different light when the adventures of the whalers are interpreted as processes of detachment from a mother imago experienced as overpowering.

A current topic of psychoanalytic discussion, at least since Wurmser's monograph (1981), is the effect of shame. This extensive monograph takes up the psychology of shame as introduced by psychoanalysis, combines it with narcissistic elements of Kohut's self-psychology and applies the concepts to Melville's literary work (Adamson, 1997). The underlying idea states that the fear of embarrassment is traced back to experiences of a massive disappointment of trust, which leads to the feeling of being let down. Melville's novel describes forms of reaction to this fear of shame. Some characters retreat, which is intensified more and more until they become socially isolated, such as the hero of the story *Bartleby the Scrivener*. Others seek revenge and destruction in order to take revenge for their shame and destroy the object of shame. The most important exponent is certainly *Moby-Dick*'s character Ahab, who wants to take revenge for the unforgettable humiliation suffered due to his amputated leg, at whatever cost it may bring about—a revenge that is re-directed to the whale. Some characters, even in *Moby-Dick*, serve only to illustrate the ultimately fatal interplay of trust, abandonment, and shame, such as the tragic figure of Pip, whose entire trust is in the captain, who nevertheless forsakes him in the water when he falls into the sea for the second time. In few figures are abandonment and shame balanced by love or care—an experience that Ahab's opponent in *Moby-Dick*, Ishmael, experiences in the encounter with Queequeg.

Certainly, the texts mentioned deserve the reader's attention; they are psychoanalytically enlightening and promote understanding of the novel's characters and the author's person. Furthermore, they show that it is inevitable that literature is interpreted according to a scholar's actual theoretical interest and horizon. An amusing example of this is the diagnosis of sleep paralysis in *Moby-Dick* (Herman, 1997). A review of older literature reveals even more foci, for example on perversion (Simpson, 1982). Earlier texts deal with the religious psychology of Melville's novels (Thompson, 1952). From an analytical point of view, however, no representation does justice to the novel's aesthetic, that is, the form of the text. Therefore, it seems reasonable to take another look at Melville, especially *Moby-Dick*.

The context: self-care, self-relativisation, identity formation

The following new attempt at interpretation is not intended to be exhaustive. Instead, its perspectivity is granted from the outset. The epistemological interest that guides my reading and interpretation of *Moby-Dick* is the question of how self-care and self-destruction interrelate with processes of identity formation. First, I explain the concept of self-care; in a second step, I provide psychoanalytic aspects of self-care and self-destruction. In the third part, I discuss the significance of the topic for identity-formation processes.

Self-care

It would be fascinating to examine how far the question of self-care—the attention that the care for oneself has attracted—is historically change-able. It would therefore be worthwhile to examine historical epochs in which self-care had a special place, at least as judged via its philosophi-cal reception, and to examine the quality of self-care changing in his-tory. One period that immediately stands out here is the post-classical period of ancient Rome—the last flowering of Roman imperialism—in the first and second centuries of our era. M. Foucault, who wrote a remarkable *History of Sexuality*, dedicated a volume to this period and titled it "le souci de soi" (1988), thereby introducing the concept of self-care or self-protection—neither of which shall be distinguished here—into the philosophical-historical debate.

From Seneca to Marcus Aurelius, the questions of how to live prop-erly and how to take care of oneself are energetically addressed again and again. The *cura sui* (*epiméleia heautoú*) becomes philosophical; pas-sionate appeals are made to the individual to free himself from external influences and fate in order to achieve a balance within himself that makes him independent of all external conditions. For this purpose, the texts mentioned above propose exercises of renunciation, of guiding one's own thoughts, and of reflection. Marcus Aurelius writes:

> How much he gains in leisure who looks not to what his neigh-bors say, or do, or intend; but considers only how his own actions may be just and holy, looking not, as Agathon says, to the moral example of others, but running a straight course and never turn-ing therefrom.
>
> (Marcus Aurelius, 2011, Book IV, 18)

What is important here is the separation of the self from the other; self-care is seen as a solitary and isolating activity.

It is noticeable that the term "self-care"—despite Foucault—has not yet attained scientific dignity, even though the problem described by the term currently has high social relevance. Social developments of de-traditionalisation and individualisation (cf. Putnam, 2000) seem to have the effect that self-care is being handed over to the individual as a task to be solved by the individual himself. An empirical indication of this is provided by the flood of guidebook literature, which accounts for the largest share of the still high turnover of the book market. Other indications are the enormous turnover rates of the cosmetics industry and the astonishing popularity and spread of the fitness wave, which emphasises physical self-care (Küchenhoff, 1998a, 2012).

If self-care becomes a social challenge, it is no wonder that many people fail to meet this challenge. The psychiatrist or psychotherapist is confronted with the clinical consequences of this failure, and new forms of psychopathological syndromes appear as a mirror of currently con-flictive living conditions. One focus of therapeutic interest has become familiar, namely, the focus on people who tend to harm themselves, to injure themselves by cutting themselves, burning cigarettes or lighters, and so on. In the beginning, these patients were viewed as hurting a sort of taboo in willingly hurting their own body. Thus, the therapist was forced to put into question what was seemingly self-evident before; sud-denly the ability to care for oneself was no longer regarded as a given, but had to be re-examined for its preconditions. This challenges us to consider the psychological capacities that are necessary to succeed in creating what seems so natural: to be good to oneself.

Psychoanalytic thoughts on self-destruction and self-care

Psychoanalytically, the concept of self-care is not explicitly elaborated, but is implicit in many constructs. The following is a brief summary of what contributes to self-care in psychodynamic terms.

Self-care is a complex personality trait which describes a certain form of good-willed, caring approach to oneself based on the most for-mative, emotionally significant, especially early biographical, relation-ship experiences. It is on this point of the intersubjective constitution of the ability to care for oneself that the great difference to the late antique concepts must be seen. Experiences in interpersonal relations are inter-nalised, and in this way, the way we deal with ourselves is a mirror of the relationship experiences we have had (cf. W. R. Bion's "containing principle"; D. W. Winnicott's "environmental mother").

Self-care is about the task of how the self can be preserved and sup-ported; self-destruction is about the self-induced endangerment of the self, that is, the inner destructive impulses that can threaten the self. This juxtaposition can easily give the impression that the two concepts are only antagonistic. At first, this seems clinically correct; self-injurious acts such as cutting the surface of one's own skin will at first appear as a basal lack of self-care. But the circumstances are not that simple; often a deeper analysis shows that the obviously destructive actions directed against one's own body also have self-care motives.

Moreover, both terms appear to be distinguished at first by quantitative differences in receiving or exerting love and destruction, meaning that if I am able to be self-caring, I give or allocate something to myself. If self-destruction supervenes, then I rob myself of something. But this would be a one-sided criterion of distinction, as if it were always more favourable for the self to receive and receive much. In contrast to this, another aspect should be brought into play, which allows for a different understanding of self-care. The thesis states that self-care also has to do with self-relativisation, which can be done in two directions—firstly with regard to the intersubjective relationship, that is, the relationship to others, but also with regard to one's own claims to completeness and perfection. According to this thesis, self-care includes the double movement of self-relativisation. But this is prerequisite for the formation of a personal identity from a psychoanalytical point of view. Thus, the thesis that self-care is connected with self-relativisation leads to the surprising finding that self-care is connected with the process of identity formation. This will be explained in more psychoanalytic detail.

The consequences of identity formation

From a psychoanalytic perspective, self-care is an ambivalent figure. It is ambivalent because "too much" self-care can be a problem in itself. If self-care is set as an exclusive goal, and therefore absolute, it can turn into an excessive occupation of the self, which can lead to narcissistic pathologies. The consequence of this excessive concern for the self is that contact to the other recedes into the background or is lost. Narcissistic pathologies are characterised by the fact that other people are used only as a means to an end (for example, to satisfy one's own needs or to stabilise oneself). Necessarily, they are accompanied by a loss of chances and qualities that may have been provided by personal relations. Others can then no longer enrich the self, and identity development is handed over to one's own person. But this loses its relevance to the other and remains one-sided or deficient.

The second form of self-relativisation addressed is that of fantasies of one's own perfection and completeness. This is also an aspect of narcissism. Self-care cannot mean cultivating fantasies of one's own perfection, but entails, conversely, being able to live with reduced inner demands, lowering the unconditional demands on oneself as well as on others and bringing them in line with reality. In other words, one aspect of self-care is to allow experiences of lack.

It has already been indicated that both aspects of self-relativisation belong together. Some psychoanalytic concepts converge at this point even though they differ in many other aspects. In developmental psychology, for example, encounters with important early caregivers significantly shape the formation of one's own identity. In the context of psychic development, it is inevitable that disappointments arise which must be processed. If the child initially harbours fantasies of inseparability and difference in the course of her early stages of life, she is forced to perceive and acknowledge other people as independent persons. The concepts of the Oedipus complex and castration anxiety have many facets and contain two very vivid challenges for psychological development. It is a matter of the child's fantasy also having to recognise the generational boundary and gender differences in the course of her development (on the concept of recognition, cf. J. Benjamin, 1995). Through both experiences, the child is confronted with irreducible differences. If development goes well, both lead to the dismantling of fantasies of perfection or omnipotence.

The development of identity is therefore bound to the continuous relativisation of one's own fantasies of perfection. Ideas of self-sufficiency, autonomy, and omnipotence are relativised or transgressed during development. If one wants to formulate this pointedly, one might say that finding identity always has to do with the acceptance of the loss of self. Or formulated even more contradictorily: only those who can lose themselves can win themselves. Those who can no longer lose themselves, those who can no longer step out of their identity role again and again because they identify too strongly with it, can become melancholy—at least that is the social psychological and role-theoretical model for the development of severe depression (Kraus, 1977).

I will now further develop this topic on the basis of the novel *Moby-Dick*.

Self-care and self-destruction in *Moby-Dick*

Moby-Dick is first and foremost an adventure novel, even if it does not exhaust itself in this function. The novel's plot quickly told: Ishmael, so the text tells us in the beginning, is looking for new possibilities of experience. He is looking for new territory, and that is why he joins the whalers, in order to find himself or to expand his world at the borders of the world, at the limits of the technical possibilities of the time, in the exceptional situation of the closed society of a whaler ship and in view of the infinite beauty of the sea. It takes some time in the novel before Ishmael actually sets off—he doesn't board the ship until the twenty-first of a total of a hundred and thirty-five chapters of the novel.

The introductory chapters show how he gradually makes contact with the whalers, and his encounter with Queequeg—a man who at first seems sinister but then becomes extremely good-natured—is described in a particularly subtle way. The subtlety rests in the interplay between the fear of the powerful, seemingly inaccessible journeyman and a somewhat homosexual fascination. The passage where Ishmael has to share a bed with him in a sailors' hotel due to lack of space is particularly noteworthy. Ishmael's fascination, his fascination with the milieu of whaling, which is a world with its own laws, but which is nevertheless increasingly becoming an allegory of the world in general; this fascination also draws the reader more and more into the events of the novel. So Ishmael hires on an old whaling ship, the *Pequod*.

Strangely enough, he, who is the first-person narrator of the novel for most of the time, and through whom we find our way into the world of travel, steps back more and more after the ship has taken off. Now the main character of the novel, if there is a single main character at all, becomes Ahab. He is the well-known one-legged captain who had to survive a fight with the legendary white whale, Moby-Dick, during an earlier fishing expedition. Soon he reveals to the crew of the *Pequod* the real mission of this whaling expedition, which all the others had undertaken for the sake of adventure or of pecuniary interests. He more or less succeeds in captivating the crew with his spleen, because after all, the search for the whale is like the proverbial search for a needle in a haystack. The spell, which also fascinates the reader, not only the crew, is created by the unbending will or unconditional determination to risk everything in one's own life for the sake of this goal, because only in this way can Ahab regain his damaged life.

The end is predestined from the beginning; nevertheless, the development remains exciting: Ahab meets the white whale at the end, the fight begins again. Finally, he goes down and drags the entire crew down with him. Only Ishmael survives by an absurd and symbolic circumstance. When the *Pequod* goes down, he is thrown into a wooden coffin, which has its own story in the book. Queequeg, the eerily friendly harpooner, whom he meets at the beginning and with whom he joins the ship, had built this coffin on the way because he thought he had to die. And so Ishmael falls into this coffin, drifts on the sea for a while, and then is the only one who is finally saved.

A first line of interpretation suggests itself: the novel has two heroes facing each other: on the one hand, Ahab the captain, who—unable to forget an insult—sacrifices his life for one idea; and on the other, Ishmael the sailor, but also narrator and only survivor. The figure of Ahab is easier to grasp than that of Ishmael. It is well known that Melville had made a good study of the psychiatric literature of the time. When the novel was published in 1851, the diagnosis of monomania was popular in psychiatry (see, e.g., Walsh, 2010). Insanity, according to psychiatric doctrine, arises from the excess or one-sided cultivation of a tendency that is taken to extremes. Playing with fire becomes pyromania, theft becomes kleptomania, the urge to move becomes poriomania, and so on. Esquirol, one of the most famous psychiatrists of the time, recognises in monomania the mental illness of the present day; he attributes it to the unilateral and individualising tendency that is inherent in early capitalist society. The state of society drives one to monomania, and monomania is the mirror image of society. Ahab is monomaniac in this way.

But who is Ishmael? He is much more difficult to determine, especially since he disappears more and more from the text and vanishes, as it were, only to reappear again towards the end. This is an artistic and stylistic tool in the novel, which allows the person to recede behind his function, as Ishmael's most important characteristic is as the narrator. (The extent to which Melville was concerned with the function and place of writing is also apparent in other texts, especially in the bizarre and Kafkaesque narrative of *Bartleby the Scrivener*, to which G. Deleuze (1997) dedicated a short monograph worth reading.) To put it bluntly, we can say that we learn the most from Ishmael by examining the structure of the text, or, to put it another way: the antagonist of Ahab is the structure of the text itself. And it is striking and adventurous enough. The book does not begin in any conventional way. Whoever opens it is first confronted with an etymology of the whale, as it says in a parenthesis of the text "supplied by a Late Consumptive Usher to a Grammar School". After this derivation of the word "whale", excerpts follow that are drawn from quotations covering the entire world literature, excerpts of passages dealing with the whale, and these excerpts are "compiled by a sub-sub-librarian". Only then does Chapter 1 follow with the writer's circumstantial introduction:

> Call me Ishmael. Some years ago—never mind how long precisely—having little or no money in my purse, and nothing particular to interest me on shore, I thought I would sail about a little and see the watery part of the world. It is a way I have of driving off the spleen and regulating the circulation. Whenever I find myself growing grim about the mouth; whenever it is a damp, drizzly November in my soul; whenever I find myself involuntarily pausing before coffin warehouses, and bringing up the rear of every funeral I meet; and especially whenever my hypos get such an upper hand of me, that it requires a strong moral principle to prevent me from deliberately stepping into the street, and methodically knocking people's hats off—then, I account it high time to get to sea as soon as I can.

So the novel begins—with a break in the traditional novel structure before the actual plot has even begun. At the beginning, there is no unified narrative, but rather, the complexity of the writing style, lexical entries, quotations, and explanations of words. This text structure is comparable to musical works, which do not begin with the introduction of a motif, but with its variation. And this text structure is retained further on. Although the narrative thread is adopted later, it is always left behind again and again. And styles follow one another with great variety. Some chapters, such as the fortieth, are structured like a drama. Others resemble scientific treatises, such as Chapter 32, which is dedicated to the zoology of whales. After Moby-Dick was introduced as a white whale, an essay immediately follows on the colour white (Chapter 42). The novel is thus anything but purposeful, and the many detours in the text become more important than the progress of the plot. The text loses itself in the side tangents, in interspersed narratives that can stand on their own. But this text structure belongs to the essence of the novel. If the digressions, the transgressions, and meanderings in the text are cut out for the purpose of a children's edition or for the purpose of a film adaptation, in order to make the book merely a seafaring novel, then the novel is reduced entirely to one side. Then there is only Ahab and the white whale, and the counterweight formed by Ishmael or the formal structure of the text is lost.

The digressions interspersed throughout the text are also striking in another way in relation to the plot. The text communicates with other historically significant literary works, and the book is impregnated with an exuberant intertextuality (Kristeva, 1984). The text has references in all directions, and not only in the digressions. The Bible, and especially the Apocalypse, come into play on more than one occasion, such as when Moby-Dick is described as Leviathan. Even the names of the two heroes, Ahab and Ishmael, are taken from the Old Testament; Ahab is a king of Israel, and Ishmael is the prototype of the individual who was cast out of the religious community by God and must continue to live on his own. Then again, Ahab's soliloquies are carried by Shakespearean language, such that the texts could come from a royal drama (cf. Chapter 37):

> Dry heat upon my brow? Oh! time was, when as the sunrise nobly spurred me, so the sunset soothed. No more. This lovely light, it lights not me; all loveliness is anguish to me, since I can ne'er enjoy. Gifted with the high perception, I lack the low, enjoying power; damned, most subtly and most malignantly! damned in the midst of Paradise! Good night—good night! (Waving his hand, he moves from the window.)

'Twas not so hard a task. I thought to find one stubborn, at the least; but my one cogged circle fits into all their various wheels, and they revolve. Or, if you will, like so many ant-hills of powder, they all stand before me; and I their match. Oh, hard! that to fire others, the match itself must needs be wasting! What I've dared, I've willed; and what I've willed, I'll do! They think me mad—Starbuck does; but I'm demoniac, I am madness maddened! That wild madness that's only calm to comprehend itself! The prophecy was that I should be dismembered; and—Aye! I lost this leg. I now prophesy that I will dismember my dismemberer.

Some comparisons, spun across lines in the text, cannot be read other than as Homeric comparisons. The fact that the voyage of the *Pequod* begins in Nantucket is itself an allusion. Shortly before, a novel essential to American literature is published, also an adventure and shipping novel, *The Adventures of Arthur Gordon Pym*, written by Edgar Allan Poe, whose adventures also begin in Nantucket.

What does this text structure teach? It shows us two things: it tells us something about Ishmael as a representative of the text, but it also tells us—and this may now seem paradoxical—something about the proximity between Ishmael and Ahab.

Ishmael's identity is revealed to the reader in the same way as the text is revealed. Reading here means picking up or collecting, identity is not predetermined, rather, it is only formed as the text progresses. When reading, the reader does not know what to expect next. Heterogeneity takes the place of unambiguity. The identity of the novel unfolds as a process, not as the deductive unfolding of predetermined characteristics. The monomaniacal goal orientation of the hero Ahab is replaced by the creativity of detours. In that the form of the written text constitutes the identity of the person, reference is made to the significance of writing for the formation of identity. Mind you, this is not a novel of the twentieth or twenty-first century that speaks to a postmodern arbitrariness. It is quite obvious that the novel's claim is to depict the emergence of a concept of the world; it is a novel of education, a novel of self-realisation processes, which at the same time attempts to capture the world of its time in allegorical attempts at interpretation. This claim must be taken seriously (see below).

But first of all, the contrast between Ahab, on the one hand, and the text structure, on the other, could not be greater. Ishmael and the text are agile, committed to heterogeneity, thus flexible; Ishmael survives through this. Ahab, on the other hand, is great, even oversized. He casts a spell over everyone and knows how to swear the crew to his goals, despite all warnings and reservations (the novel gives impressive descriptions of mass psychological phenomena). The novel juxtaposes the monomania of one-sided goal orientation with the dissemination of form. It contrasts defiant self-discovery at all costs, which carries death within itself, with the play of references and experiential connections. Thus, two modes of self-realisation are presented here. The one can be described as single-mindedness at any price, contrasted with the meandering development, which is not aimless, and which not only accepts detours, but is formed and shaped by them, which thus never imagines reaching its goal on its own and from within, without reference, without articulation with others.

This is the art of the novel: Ishmael, as a person, cannot be the counter-hero to Ahab, because this would not introduce anything new. The struggle of the giants would remain stuck on the same level as a struggle between two antagonistic principles; the conception would remain merely dualistic, like the struggle between Ahab and the whale. But that is what is obviously to be criticised and overcome. This seems to me to be an essential trick of the novel, that the alternatives are introduced from heterogeneous positions. A second hero, who does not fight but instead confronts the combative one, would be a contradiction in itself. Thus, the alternative is introduced through a "disappearance" of the subject, Ishmael, through the multiplicity of forms.

But there is one more refraction in the text. It becomes visible in the aforementioned similarity (that sounds paradoxical at first sight), in the connecting element between Ahab and Ishmael, which exists despite the fact that they are so opposed to each other. Ishmael is the first-person narrator of the novel; the author thus presents him to us as the figure in the novel who is responsible for the text. And the text itself, the testimony of this journey, which overflows in all directions, is in itself megalomaniac. Ishmael is also repeatedly subject to this megalomania of world designs, especially in his function as a novel—as a chronicler. This idea of greatness, to explain and explain the whole world in the context of a whaling novel, as it were, is taken *ad absurdum* in the novel itself. There are passages which, in my opinion, are not involuntary, but purposeful comedy. For example, the legend of St George fighting the dragon is rewritten against all evidence, so that St George actually fought a whale.

> Let not the modern paintings of this scene mislead us; for though the creature encountered by that valiant whaleman of old is vaguely represented of a griffin-like shape, and though the battle is depicted on land and the saint on horseback, yet considering the great ignorance of those times, when the true form of the whale was unknown to artists; and considering that as in Perseus' case, St. George's whale might have crawled up out of the sea on the beach; and considering that the animal ridden by St. George might have been only a large seal, or sea-horse; bearing all this in mind, it will not appear altogether incompatible with the sacred legend and the ancientest draughts of the scene, to hold this so-called dragon no other than the great Leviathan himself. In fact, placed before the strict and piercing truth, this whole story will fare like that fish, flesh, and fowl idol of the Philistines, Dagon by name; who being planted before the ark of Israel, his horse's head and both the palms of his hands fell off from him, and only the stump or fishy part of him remained. Thus, then, one of our own noble stamp, even a whaleman, is the tutelary guardian of England; and by good rights, we harpooneers of Nantucket should be enrolled in the most noble order of St. George.
>
> (Chapter 82)

Another passage with an intended comic effect is found at the end, namely the symbolically exuberant, but narratively highly mannered and hair-raising, rescue by the coffin, which, a *deus ex machina*, suddenly appears and rescues Ishmael. In these and other passages, the text's megalomania repeatedly collapses. In other words, the text itself reproduces the opposition that was described earlier between the main characters, Ahab and Ishmael. The text is a great draft of the first-person narrator, who proceeds "ahabically" and subjects the world to the theme of the whale. Through exaggeration, but also through the divergence in form already described, this attempt is repeatedly refuted. This results in a double refraction—the text itself contains the interplay between the idea of megalomania and playful non-identity. Thus, the difference between writing and the hunt for the imaginary white whale is reduced; both forms of coping can derail narcissistically. Nevertheless, in the process of writing itself, the relativisation of monomaniacal ideas of greatness is laid out. For writing is the context of reference *par excellence* (Derrida, 1959).

I could object to the juxtaposition of Ahab and Ishmael with good reason, arguing that I leave aside the title hero of the novel, the whale, who appears first of all as the actual hero of the book, which obviously is about the whale itself. But who is Moby-Dick? Only at the end of the story does it appear in the flesh—this brief appearance is not surprising. When it reveals itself, it reveals what the reader already knew, namely its uncontrollable and destructive power. It brings death to almost everyone, only to disappear again. The novel gains its tension from the anticipation of this encounter, which then contains no moments of surprise. More important than the whale itself is what the heroes of the novel think of it or read into it. And here, a significant difference becomes apparent. For Ishmael, it is not the one whale that is decisive, but the world of whales, whale watching is his interpretation of the world, whaling is the condition of spontaneity, freedom, and inventiveness (cf. Fluck, 1997, p. 237). For Ahab, there is only one whale—Moby-Dick. With it, he violates the laws of whaling, namely that every whale one meets should be caught (Deleuze, 1997). But why is it the one whale? Long before Moby-Dick appears, in the already mentioned central Chapter 42, the text says who Moby-Dick is. He is introduced as a symbol, more precisely, as a symbol of a symbol, namely the colour white. The colour white, however, is characterised in ever new attempts in this decidedly iridescent and creative chapter as "the incomprehensible", but also as "the horror":

> I know that, to the common apprehension, this phenomenon of
> whiteness is not confessed to be the prime agent in exaggerating
> the terror of objects otherwise terrible; nor to the unimagina-
> tive mind is there aught of terror in those appearances whose

awfulness to another mind almost solely consists in this one phenomenon, especially when exhibited under any form at all approaching to muteness or universality.

The strangely uncanny whiteness finally is the "monumental white shroud that wraps all the prospect around him. And of all these things the Albino whale was the symbol."

The white whale is thus not another hero, not an antagonist, but a symbol; it is the object of the search for identity, but the object that eludes it and which no one can seize, and which, precisely because it is beyond all attribution, attracts phantasms. Melville has masterfully portrayed this transcendental function; in the novel, everything revolves around the white whale, but it is introduced as a mystery, and it only appears in reality at the end of the book and is destructive precisely because it rejects all appropriation.

Search for identity and de-identification

The decisive statement of the text seems to me to lie in the interplay between the idea of greatness and playful non-identity described above. A simple psychoanalytical interpretation could also be that Ahab is a traumatically stressed person. He would then—and there are certainly good reasons for this line of interpretation—derive the merciless revenge of the captain from his "castration". He has had the experience of traumatic loss: the whale has bitten his leg off, and he cannot come to terms with it. He wants to rebuild himself, to create his identity again and again by attacking the aggressor, killing the murderer. Ahab therefore remains caught up in narcissism and cannot integrate the lack into his identity. The absence of his leg becomes his anchor point in the world; this is portrayed in a very powerful way by the fact that Ahab, with his prosthetic leg not accidentally carved out of whale bones, repeatedly fixes himself in a recess in the deck of the *Pequod*.

This interpretation is correct, but it still falls short of what is required, compared to other patterns of interpretation mentioned in the introduction. It explains—this is the first point—nothing of the fascination that seizes the reader, even if, like me, one is not particularly interested in whaling or adventure novels. In my opinion, the reader inevitably undertakes a de-pathologisation. He recognises himself, sometimes against his will, in Ahab. For a member of the university, for example, it seems obvious to take up the "ahabism" of scientific career planning. Sometimes it seems that the prerequisite for a scientific career is to stop playing games, as if blinkers or binoculars were the only optical aids that were suitable for a victory in a scientific career. But we also know "ahabism" in relationships, where it always plays a role. After all, it is not bad to carry the other person along when you are enthusiastic yourself. The limit is where only the captain has the say and all other goals have to stay behind.

We know from psychoanalysis or from working with children how important the function of play is. Playing with things, with words, with perspectives always means learning to see something with different eyes. The change of perspective is an indispensable prerequisite for our self-care. We have to do it very often, but we cannot always be what we pretend to be or how we stage ourselves. "Ahabism" in dealing with oneself also means identifying with the image of one's self, to freeze in a certain way and only in this self-image. Then it becomes impossible to allow surprise and uncertainty—the productive questioning in one's own life.

But even this perspective falls short. It is worth recalling the analysis of the double refraction in the novel: the opposition of identity and disidentification, of Ishmael and Ahab, reproduces itself in the text and has a place, as it were, in the writing process itself—namely as a pendulum swinging between the idea of greatness of the design and the diversification of the text. But in this way, this opposition is de-pathologised and normalised. The described interplay, as the novel seems to express it, belongs to human fate, at least to one that is organised in Western societies and according to the competitive rules of our capitalistic economy. In this interpretation, Ahab would be an allegory of human consciousness, of a consciousness in which ideas of identity are formed, necessarily and unavoidably, and where consciousness always tends to be absolute, to exaggerate itself, and to engage in deadly power struggles with others, which are characterised by building one's own existence on the struggle and the need to win. This consciousness, however, is undermined—and it must be undermined—by all the experiences outside of these self-designs, through connections, references, and marginal perspectives outside the centred gaze. Allowing this undermining movement to interfere is what allows Ishmael to survive in the novel. Because he ever so often falls back into his own conception of greatness, he cannot understand himself completely and cannot grasp the causes for his own survival, especially as a chronicler of the text; the sobbing story of falling into Queequeg's coffin is a sign of this. This story is a dramatisation and exaggeration of the reason for survival, which actually allows for the detour and, in the end, playfulness. The reason for Ishmael's salvation lies in writing. He is the writer, that is, the one who, in the process of writing, can be content with the fact that not everything is said with one word, that all reality cannot be captured with one object. The white whale, finally, stands for this object, which escapes and is not challenged without punishment.

In my opinion, the novel has something to do with the distinction made by the French psychoanalyst Lacan (2006), the distinction between the imaginary, the symbolic, and the real. For Lacan, the real is the impossible, that is, that which cannot be grasped in one's own imagination, in one's own wishful thinking, but also in speaking or thinking, in any form of psychological representation. The most blatant and impressive example of this reality is the experience of death, which determines us all, but which we cannot imagine. But the real can also be the withdrawing personality of the other, beyond the image we form of him, which is masterfully represented by the white whale. With Lacan, the imaginary is what we imagine. And these imagined images tend to make us conceited. The imaginary world tends towards the idea of greatness, as it is presented in the novel by Ahab. All these conscious imaginings that we take over into our ego or ego-consciousness are self-conceptions that are constantly exceeded by unconscious desire. This is not simply natural, but is formed by structures of meaning, by the symbolic.

The conscious intention or desire for perfection, for omnipotence over reality, or for self-sufficiency or autarky is answered by this diversity—this interconnectedness of desire, which cannot be explained and satisfied from one point. But there is not the one and only one possibility; rather, identity is shaped by this interplay of determination and distraction, of identification and dis-identification. This does not mean aimlessness, just as the novel has a narrative strand, but it does mean the constant relativisation of one's own inexorability. This creates a moment of freedom, which, following in Lacan's footsteps, Hermann Lang has described very beautifully:

> But this … gives us a moment of freedom—an openness that is the prerequisite for losing oneself in ever new identifications, for slipping into ever new roles, for being able to build up a supposedly identical ego—a freedom that at the same time offers possibilities for questioning this imaginary construct.
>
> (Lang, 1980, p. 201; translated for this edition)

CHAPTER 4

Time and the other in the process of remembering—*Embers* (S. Márai)

Sándor Márai's novel *Embers* was published in 1942. It fell into oblivion for decades and was barely received, at least in non-Hungarian countries. So, the novel's fate could be a worthwhile subject of an analysis that deals with forgetting and remembering literature. Indeed, it is an interesting question why a novel disappears from public interest only to be translated into English and German again after almost fifty years, with the effect of being acclaimed and compared with the works of Proust, Mann, or Joyce. Is it publishing skill, is it business calculation, is it the revision of an historical injustice owed to the consequences of the Second World War and exile (Zeltner, 2001), or does the novel address socially significant issues today much more so than in days past, which results in the new edition's success today? Arguably, it is precisely these dynamics that have to be taken into account when dealing with processes of remembering. Everything in this book seems to be directed backwards—the life world, the language (as far as it is authentically reproduced in the translation), and the content. Is this nostalgic side part of its topicality (Gauss, 2001)? After all, this is a book that was written in Hungary in 1942!

The novel deals with the elucidation of the past, or more precisely, with the meticulous reconstruction of an evening forty-one years ago and its lifelong precursors and effects. The general, Henrik, lives in a castle; he receives the news that an old friend, Konrad, wants to visit him. They were intimately connected: "Their friendship was deep and wordless, as are all the emotions that will last a lifetime" (p. 36). Nevertheless, they are quite opposite personalities, one of them representing the love of order, conversation, and rationality, the other, the guest, is the advocate of music, passion, and entanglement. The novel centres on a conversation Konrad and Henrik had one evening and the chances to recall the past. Konrad hardly speaks during this evening, which is the novel's present tense, but nevertheless induces Henrik to unfold his life story—his memories. Details are recalled meticulously, all descriptions revolve around central questions, which are nonetheless held in suspense and not explicitly answered: did Konrad have a passionate relationship with Henrik's wife Chrisztina at the time? Did he cheat him, even try to kill him just before the evening all three saw each other for the last time, only to leave Henrik and the castle forever the next day? Chrisztina remains living on the same estate as Henrik, but does not speak to or see her husband for eight years, until her death.

In some respects, the novel's process of remembering is comparable to the analytical situation, it seems. To begin with, there is a similar form of reconstructing the past via conversation as a communicative setting in which one, the guest, is usually silent, but the host unfolds his or her memories, set in an asymmetrical dialogue situation. Obviously, Konrad's presence triggers memory processes. In addition, the novel impressively describes a staging: both friends who at first were so closely connected then completely distanced, meet each other with the highest emotional intensity, and between them a drama of love and death, of guilt and atonement, of perpetration and sacrifice is created, without it always being clear who plays which role.

But comparability with the analytical situation has its limits. The author (1) never leaves a doubt that the consequence of this re-encounter is death, not life or future. Both Konrad and Henrik have lived only for this moment, beyond which there will be no more life for either of them. This also means, however, that (2) the re-encounter is affectively charged in such a way that it cannot be relativised, although all attempts at remembrance seem to aim at it. There is nothing beyond this present relationship—it is not a means but an end, and an end in itself. In other words, the history of a relationship is reconstructed, but at the same time it is staged ("acted in"), and this staging itself cannot be reflected upon. The subtle memory of the events forty-one years ago does not really become the past, because in the present relationship there is nothing that can really make this past part of the past. Using Freud's terminology, one could say that remembrance work, but not mourning work, is done, if remembrance work is understood as the mental effort that allows memories to be released, but mourning work would be the mental work that allowed the remembrance object to be detached or distanced. In this case, precisely because memory is not set in relation to the present *hic* and *nunc*, it does not allow the remembered to become the past. That which has in fact passed by for so long continues to have an effect, it has been preserved for forty-one years, and it is repeated that evening. The undissolved bond of both friends is held onto at all costs, even at the price of death. Remembering is performed with the aim to negate the present: instead of mourning, it is not melancholy but resignation that takes the place of sadness; nothing can be forgotten here, nothing can likewise be forgiven, and so the future is also destroyed. The process of remembrance confirms what linguistic form and the way of life depicted in the novel already express, namely that the lifestyle of an aristocrat who grew up in the Habsburg imperial and royal monarchy has survived, but still nothing is allowed in to take its place.

But what quality does the memory have then? Does it fail? Or wouldn't it be more correct to say that the novel describes a process of remembering that is in a certain sense "abuse of memory" (Todorov, 1995)? By persistently excluding the presence of the people who remember, nothing new is created from memory. On the contrary, working on the past prevents reviewing the present. The reason for the abuse of memory in the novel lies nowhere else to be found than in the relationship between the two protagonists. Konrad listens, is mostly silent, and his silence inspires Henrik's memories, but what is missing is an answer—not only the factual answer, but the emotional resonance. The reader thus becomes an ambivalent observer of a relationship that bears witness to dominance and submission, love and contempt, fusion and death, and against which Henrik's reflected psychological analyses have no chance at all. None of the protagonists steps out of his role, as there is no third party to which both could refer. The time interval has not created a (personal, emotional) distance, and as such, the protagonists cannot adopt a self-distanced stance comparable to the therapeutic ego split in analysis, which would allow each to see in the other, the respective other in their conversation, something more than an object of one's own desires. This brings about the consequence that both would no longer be absorbed in the object status, so that one could interpret the object desire from a point of view beyond the object status. That there is no third party here, that there never was a third party between them, is apparent through Chrisztina, who, as a woman, is only an object between two men. She does not have a life of her own, at least the novel does not report on it. She is exploited by the men and used for a specific psychic function, that is, to break up the lifetime prison that forms this male love. But she won't succeed in doing so.

It deserves attention that even language, the finely chiselled words, the most vivid descriptions, do not have the power to serve as a third party—perhaps because it remains a monologue and cannot become a real exchange of words. The critical interpretation given here would have to be proven in an in-depth formal analysis of the novel, which cannot be done at this point. It would have to prove that no mediation appears in the obvious antagonism between the novel's closed epic structure and the melancholically beautiful, poetic language, on the one hand, and the dramatic content, on the other. In any case, my proposition is that the form conjures up bourgeoisie in the best sense and that it persists, even where dramatic actions debunk it. The novel does not really take sides, but rather exhibits painful contradictions.

One hour of analysis

How do we imagine—in contrast to the novel—the process of remembering in the psychoanalytic cure? In the following section, a small, admittedly isolated, piece of empirical material will show how memory is used in psychoanalysis. I will therefore briefly report on an hour of analysis. (Perhaps, and this is important to note, my desire colours the process; perhaps I, who am on the trail of memory, remember differently than usual?) I will not present a casual report as a whole, but rather a small piece of memory work, as it is possible in the psychoanalytic process.

To understand the following, it is only necessary to know in advance that after two weeks of interruption of the analysis during the Christmas and New Year period, the patient comes back for her first session in the New Year. She greets me in a friendly way and reports first that she felt somehow uncomfortable before the hour, without being able to explain it properly. She had not really known whether she wanted to come at all. Following her associations, she then reports that circumstances had indeed made it difficult for her to come. She had parked her car in an underground garage, it had been broken into—three other cars as well—she didn't know whether to file a complaint, whether to inform the parking garage attendant, or whether she should hurry up to come to analysis. All her belongings had been rummaged through, but it was important for her to be here. She wanted to ask me what I meant by my last remark I made at the end of the session before Christmas, when I just said that the session was over and we won't see each other for two weeks; whether I wanted to indicate to her that she had done something wrong, whether she should have taken up the goodbye, and so on.

Thoughts follow that she is doing well, that she would be travelling a lot soon, whom she would like to visit, and so forth. No more vacations are arranged between us; she says nothing about how the analysis would be affected by her plans. I feel abandoned, treated interchangeably, and I have the feeling that the patient is triumphing over me, that she is showing me that she does not need me and that she did not mind the separation. In my own associations on the patient's material, I combine the various impressions, the description of her fear of the session, the description of her own distress, that her car was broken into, that she was in distress and overwhelmed, but then also the suddenly different mood, her expansiveness. I suggest to her to consider the way she comes back into the analysis after an interruption and immediately thinks again about how she could leave, in connection with the feelings of fear and being overwhelmed expressed at the beginning. In order not to be at the mercy of being alone, she quickly turned the situation around. She doesn't explicitly go into this, but tells a little story from her skiing vacation, that she was left behind in the village by her skiing friend because she doesn't like skiing; she didn't want to meet him for lunch either, she didn't mind being alone for the day. But that's not the most important thing: she wanted to discuss something else with me, namely that last Saturday, already back from vacation, she visited a cousin with whom she would have fallen in love if he wasn't her cousin, who totally understood her, with whom she felt as one, whom she must always think about now. She is frightened by herself, the love for her boyfriend could be a sudden mistake, maybe he wants to leave her suddenly. I point out to her that this idea could be read as a comment on my interpretation and add that she obviously fears nothing more than this sudden loss, as if a contact, even a long and good one, could break off abruptly and completely. She begins to think that it is especially so on Saturdays but does not understand it at all. Then it occurs to her that in the hospital, which she had to visit often as a little girl because of a chronic childhood illness, there were no visiting hours on Saturdays, that she feared nothing as much as these days, where there were no visitations by the doctors, but where she could not go to the other children either, like on all other days, because of constant infusions. So, Saturday was the day of loneliness, of the loss of any link—a fate she did not understand at the time but only endured as a catastrophic breaking-in. (In the next few sessions, she remembers her cousin's name, shares the two initial letters of my first name, Jo, a linguistic connection that puts the cousin in the place of the absent analyst, who may then become superfluous.)

This excerpt of a therapy session that is not further contextualised is intended to characterise the place of the other in the analysis. First of all, my presence is important; through this presence, which at the same time opens up space, I become the addressee of conscious fears, but also of unconscious entanglements via the transference. Second, by being present, I create a therapeutic space, a transitional space in the sense of D. W. Winnicott (1953), in which an unconscious relational form not known and not amenable to mere reflection can first of all be represented. And third, this transferential space includes making one's own perception available, just as I feel in this hour that I am being treated interchangeably, that I am being left behind. My countertransference feelings complete the emotional content of the unconscious scene.

But the case is not settled with this statement. Now it is, in the first place, important to connect the different perceptions of what is heard, felt, known from earlier hours with the aim of grasping what currently shapes the relationship between us. Only then does the following become clear: first, the complete cognitive-affective characteristics of our shared present—the fear of being left behind and the search for a forced independence are closely linked. Second, the discrepancy between the conscious thought that an interruption of the analysis is not important and the violent emotional reaction to it becomes apparent. At this point, the interpretation bridges both, and then the actual scene can in turn be linked to pivotal data of the life story: the patient was severely small when she was born and, as a consequence, had to spend several months during her first year of life in the incubator, and she was repeatedly readmitted to hospital later on. The feeling of the sudden breakdown of the relationship was a hint of that atrocious experience. Thus, time is created, as it were, as the present starts to be differentiated from the past, and this emerging difference allows new narratives to develop, such as ideas concerning more situations of loneliness. The analyst and the analysand can work out further self-descriptions together, so if the analysand thinks of herself now that her self-image has been one-sided, she always had considered herself to be the spoiled one, the choosy princess, but now she realises that she also is the small one, the fearful one, the one who is easily thrown into a panic.

Some conclusions

Place of the other

The place of the other has already been described as a presence, as a guarantor of a transitional space, as a partner affectively involved in interaction and as an interpreter; these characteristics are used to describe divergent positions that fit into an area of presence and absence, of proximity and distance. To summarise this double movement, the place of the other can be understood as one of triangulation or one of playing with difference. Thus, the other, the analyst, is on the one hand a participant in the game of staging, addressee of this staging, object of desire, participating in the process with their own desire, but the analyst is also the one who distances him- or herself from this object relationship again, who creates links using his or her interpretive activity. The analyst introduces a double difference—first, the difference between the object and the other: the analyst is the object of transference, and at the same time the one who is not identical with this object; he or she is the person who distances him- or herself from the role ascribed them. Second, by disappointing unconscious expectations, the analyst introduces a moment of lack that enables or necessitates thinking: they do not act in the intended role of the object or satisfy this expectation.

It is important that the analyst is emotionally present as an other in order to make the disappointment of unconscious desire bearable. The presence of the analyst mentioned in the last section is also an emotional presence; the experiences of difference must be endured, and this is only possible in a protective environment that does not deny the lack but embeds it, as it were. The presence of the object is determined by proximity and distance at the same time; both too much proximity and too much distance prevent the formation of experiences in the analysis. These spatial metaphors could also be reformulated using temporal images, in which case, one must speak of a developmental delay. Here, the same rules apply in analysis as in child development; if the object remains away too long for the infant, who does not yet have the internalised certainty that the object is not lost even after it has disappeared, then the object link can be lost—the image of the object itself is lost. If it never leaves, the *Fort–Da* game cannot initiate the process of symbolisation.

The introduction of difference creates temporality

Through both differences between object and other, and between desire and satisfaction, the analyst introduces temporality. The experience of time arises from the experience of difference. The experiential presence in the analysis itself is temporally structured by the delay. And by showing in the analysis that desire is not only directed at the current relationship partner, but that another, life-historically fixed object is superimposed on the current one, the difference also refers to past sources of the experience. This means, however, that temporality does not arise from the externally imposed inclusion of the past, but rather from the processing of the present relationship. In the shared and affectively significant present, the past is in a way extricated out of the present with the help of the special position of the other. The goal of memory in the analysis is thus not merely to awaken the past, but to create the past in general.

Remembering work and mourning work

The past is created in two ways: *memory work* aims to release memories against the resistance that opposes consciousness. It is, as Paul Ricœur pointed out in his wonderful book *The Enigma of the Past* (Ricœur, 1998), at the same time *mourning work*. Mourning, however, consists, as we have known since Freud's work on "Mourning and melancholia" (Freud, 1917e), of detaching oneself from the object, thereby creating distance. Memory work and mourning work come together, in which the process of memory work can resolve the emotional relationship to the object. Merleau-Ponty (1962, p. 85) spoke of the "former present that cannot decide to recede into the past". Mourning work has the effect of letting go of an object in its affective significance and thus allowing it to become a past object. Mourning work should not be cognitively trivialised. It is a painful process that enables or forces the experiential differences described above. Whether this mourning work also has an aggressive side needs to be examined, for the affective and temporal distance from the object requires forced distancing. In any case, Winnicott (1969) held the destructive impulse responsible for the fact that the outside can arise at all. When he writes that in every successful analysis the situation must be lived through, that the analyst is destroyed by the analysand, but that the analyst must survive the destruction, he means that object and other can only separate in this way. It is a painful process that releases the object from the illusion of omnipotent disposition, in order to then use it and be able to perceive it as "other"—its alterity is confirmed only when the object survives. What does this mean concretely for the analysis, for the case study mentioned? If I had felt insulted by the patient's efforts to be self-sufficient, through her wish to skip the analysis sessions, and had withdrawn in minute emotional reactions, or if I had responded rigidly and moralisingly, then I would not have survived as an analyst, and a mourning process would have been impossible. Winnicott stresses that survival in this context means "not retaliate" (Winnicott, 1969, p. 714).

Forgiveness as radicalised mourning

Ricœur (1998) has particularly emphasised another aspect of mourning: forgiveness. Ricœur distinguishes "heavy forgiveness" or "difficult forgiveness" from all light, insignificant forms of forgiveness. Psychoanalytically speaking, it belongs to what Melanie Klein calls the depressive position. "Heavy forgiveness" does not serve to balance outstanding accounts, to erase a debt, but rather, as Ricœur says, to "untangle knots". He describes two knots that are directly relevant to psychoanalysis. The first is the knot of insoluble conflicts, of irrevocable disputes. In fact, every analysis comes up against such insoluble and tragic conflicts, such as when the patient's mother had to hand her over to the clinic postpartum to keep her alive, a step that is then inevitably processed not as a rescue but as an abandonment. Secondly, Ricœur describes the knot of irreparable damage and crime. In the analysis, these accounts are important on two sides—it is relevant to the suffering that has been inflicted on traumatised people, for example, but also to what has been done to others through their own fault. Mere forgetting only denies these knots; they must be named—as fate or as guilt—and accepted in their insolubility. Only then, when the analysand is able to face the severe damage in childhood without reproach, but to see as well how many people she has harmed for the sake of the enormous fear of dependence, only then will the work of mourning be complete. Ricœur expressed this wonderfully: "accepting the unpaid debt; accepting that one is and remains an insolvent debtor; accepting that there is loss; mourning the debt itself". The consequence of this is: "The past is—I add: then—really outdated: for its 'no longer being' causes no more suffering; its 'having been' regains its honor" (Ricœur, 1998, p. 155; translated for this edition). Exactly this forgiveness is missing in Márai's novel *Embers*.

Too much and too little memory

Ricœur is certainly also right in saying that the separation of the past from the present fails when there is too much, but also when there is too little memory. "The too much or too little of memory has the same shortcoming, however, namely that the past is attached to the present: 'the past that does not pass away', which some contemporary historians speak of" (Ricœur, 1998, p. 113). This observation can be transferred well to the analytical situation. Too little memory, according to the model of repression for which we have given an example, is valid if an experience has remained virulent, that is, has never passed, but rather has retained its effect, so that it has been forgotten but not disappeared. This is the psychology of neurosis that is based on the defence principle of repression.

The fact that there is too little memory is also encountered clinically today in a more radicalised way, namely when memory must be erased in every form, when the trace that leads—by whatever means—to the never-ending past is erased. This describes not only a gradual, but also a qualitative difference: too little memory then means that not only the conscious memory is erased, but also the unconscious representation, to put it simply, is destroyed. What remains is, for example, the hallucination of emptiness, as André Green (1993) describes it in his interpretation of "white psychosis"; what remains is the lack of imagination that characterises some psychosomatic patients. Both use a defence mechanism that Lacan (1958) has worked out: foreclosure that denies any access to the representation of an experience at all.

On the other hand, there is also the excess of memory, when it is not possible to repress experience, where the consciousness cannot turn away from past experiences, where the experienced, as a flashback of a traumatic return, always breaks into conscious experience anew. I prefer to speak of recurrence and distinguish it from repetition (Küchenhoff, 1998b), as it is conceived in Freudian psychoanalysis, because traumatic experiences or fragments of traumatic experiences often return in a very unprocessed way, whereas neurosis repetition produces processed repetitions. The difference is important; Green describes it pointedly in relation to temporality as follows: once it is a matter of "hors temps", of "out-of-time", whereby time here means the chronological time of consciousness—the neurotic experience. In repetition, it proves to be a variation of the past that is rich in associations and thus already a symbolised processing, that is, it has its own temporality, which could be characterised as a cyclical time experience (Küchenhoff & Warsitz, 2012). In contrast, the time of traumatisation is a counter-time, anti-temps.

> The deadly compulsion to repeat [sc. the recurrence, J. K.] places the analyst in a dangerous counter-transference position, where the greatest risk is to be stuck in the course of the sessions, due to the stagnation effects of endless recurrence, so that the analysis dawns into boredom. The object has always been there, but could not appear from different perspectives, since it was not only inscribed in an out-of-time, but in a counter-time.
>
> (Green, 2000, p. 147)

The damage is performed again in the present with a minimum of a new fashioning. Time is stopped; there is no difference, and this in at least three ways: there is no temporal difference, the cut into the skin makes the traumatic overwhelming an event of the present; there is no metaphorical difference, no difference that would be created by the process of symbolisation—the trauma cannot be told. And there is no difference between object and other: the therapist who, for example, causes an offence with a remark, and thus becomes the aggressor, is no longer an object of transference, a third party, but the return of the tormentor, a revenant, a ghost in the sense of Ibsen's play.

It is important to me to hold on to the commonality of too much and too little of memory. In both cases, although for different reasons, one does not succeed in freeing the present from memory; on the one hand, it is about the liberation *of* memories (from repression), but on the other hand, it is about the liberation *from* memories (which push into consciousness).

Regaining actual experiences is decisive for the real injury, for example in traumatisation. Here, the analyst as an other has an additional and specific task—he or she becomes a witness who names the (traumatic) reality and thereby makes it visible. As a witness, he or she names what he has experienced, thus introducing language and difference where it has not had a place before. But where the object of desire is to be made visible, not only is the real event remembered, but also the past horizons of expectation (to use this term by Koselleck, 1995, which is used in the historical sciences), unfulfilled wishes of the past—and not even only those of the subject, but even the wishes of others anchored in the unconscious. Here, memory becomes one that investigates every implantation of the other's desire into one's own self. Psychoanalysts such as Jean Laplanche (1988) or Horst-Eberhard Richter (1962) have brought forward this courageous idea. Both objects of memory belong to what Freud called "psychic reality". In both cases, the goal is the same: the separation of the present from the past.

Temporality of the memory process

Psychoanalysis has a radical standpoint concerning the relationship between temporality and memory. If there are unconscious memories, and the unconscious is timeless, as Freud never tires of emphasising, then this means quite specifically for memories that they are part of the present, and that they are there where the subject knows nothing of them. Augustine had already spoken of the presence of the past, the presence of the present and the presence of the future, and he referred to the presence of time modes in consciousness: "Sunt enim haec in anima tria quaedam et alibi ea non video, praesens de praeterito memoria, praesens de praesentibus contuitus, praesens de futuris expectatio" (Augustine, 2016, p. 230, Liber XI, Caput XX). For the unconscious experience, it is characteristic that *contuitus* and *memoria*, memory and contemplation, are confounded. Everything takes place in a present but disordered manner in the present representation of the time axes. The time gap, the perspective on the past, must then first be established as described.

But the memory process by which past and present experience can separate is itself temporally structured. Ricœur is right when he emphasises that memory does not refer only to time, but also needs time. In psychoanalysis, this is true in a specific and concise sense. The process of memory itself has a peculiar temporal structure; the time of memory in psychoanalysis needs time precisely because the process of memory cannot be simply planned. It needs the *kairós*, the right moment in which different experiences come together, the affective attunement to one another in the hour when the conscious descriptions and associations, speech and counter-speech, in analysis crystallise, as it were, into what Stern et al. (1998) have called a "now moment" that develops into a "moment of encounter". "In our conceptualisation, 'now moments' are a special kind of 'present moment', one that gets lit up subjectively and affectively, pulling one more fully into the present" (Stern et al., 1998, p. 911).

The most intriguing now moments arise when the patient does something that is difficult to categorise, something that demands a different and new kind of response with a personal signature that shares the analyst's subjective state (affect, phantasy, real experience etc.) with the patient. If this happens, they will enter an authentic "moment of meeting". During the "moment of meeting" a novel intersubjective contact between them will become established, new in the sense that an alteration in the "shared implicit relationship" is created. A now moment that is therapeutically seized and mutually realised is a "moment of meeting".

(p. 913)

Jacques Lacan had spoken of a "time to understand"—it is not the enduring time that always and permanently remains, but a momentary combination of levels of experience in a moment that can have a mutative, that is, changing effect, in so far as it releases new dimensions of experience. "The time for comprehending can be reduced to the instant of the glance, but this glance can include in its instant all the time needed for comprehending" (Lacan, 1945, p. 168). Analysis needs time. In the analytical process, it is necessary to give each other time, to have time, so that such moments can happen. In an historical situation where time is an increasingly scarce resource, especially in health care, the demand for time has become a political demand. An evening or a night is not enough, as the novel *Embers* shows. Memory under time pressure is based on confessions, and these lead to revenge, not forgiveness.

CHAPTER 5

Intercultural violence and intercultural transitional spaces: construction and deconstruction of the foreign—*Tracks* (L. Erdrich)

The concept of interculturalism can be misunderstood—linguistically, it pretends that there are cultural areas separate from each other which at the most can be related or linked to each other. The all too justified criticism of the concept "clash of civilizations" (Huntington, 1996) has made it clear that it is a thought trap (Sen, 2006) and highly politically explosive to understand cultural areas as distinct units. Cultural areas interpenetrate each other, since the boundaries between them are imaginary and always ideologically motivated. Nevertheless, even if they are imaginary, violence is ignited at their borders. This is where psychoanalysis comes in. Thanks to psychoanalysis, we know about the violence that makes close and intimate relationships difficult, and about the process of demarcation that often resembles a tightrope walk. The basic assumption underlying the following thought is as follows: it is possible to build a bridge from the dynamics of intimate relationships to the dynamics of intercultural violence.

This chapter deals with the construction of the foreign and the contribution of psychoanalysis to enlighten it in intercultural relations. How much this contribution is worth, the perspective on intercultural violence, should be a touchstone for this. The chapter is divided into three sections. The first part describes two corresponding mechanisms of border demarcation, the construction of the foreign and the construction of one's own identity from a psychoanalytical perspective, with the aim of developing a concept that allows one to formulate a critique of violence. The second part deals with complementary mechanisms, that is, questioning boundaries and thus preventing or overcoming violence, and of these, two metaphors crucial to psychoanalytic activity come into play—the metaphor of the transitional space and of translation. In a concluding third part, the function of literary texts to create transcultural transitional spaces and to function as translating texts will be described on the basis of the novel *Tracks* by the American author Louise Erdrich (1988).

Demarcating boundaries: the construction of the foreign and one's own identity

Psychoanalysis is useful in examining the clichés and concepts of the enemy that are directed against persons from other cultures. It is one of the basic concerns of psychoanalysis to uncover the mechanisms that cause aspirations that are not consciously recognised for oneself to be shifted or projected unconsciously from the self onto the object. These mechanisms are effective in the psyche of the individual, but they also play a role in groups and in the encounters between different societies and cultures.

In the analysis of projection, psychoanalysis provides answers to the question of how difference is created—how the foreign is constructed in the first place.

Freud, in his short text on negation (1925h), created decisive preconditions for this model. The text elaborates the constitutive function of negation. In the case of the youngest child, negation refers to perception, and even to the constitution of the inside and outside in general. It is not only a function of language and conflict, but also the "the original process by which the ego took things into itself or expelled them from itself, according to the pleasure principle" (Freud, 1925h, p. 239). At the same time, it is thus a prerequisite for the development of structures of perception and experience. The negation thus determines whether our impressions belong to us or whether they are to be regarded as part of external reality. What is decisive is that Freud emphasises that this process takes place according to the pleasure principle, and that means that from the very beginning, the judgement of reality is connected with affects. What is good remains—according to the pleasure principle—in the ego; what is bad is attributed to the outside world. The dichotomy of inside and outside becomes the dichotomy of inside/good–outside/bad. The affect—and this is the provocative message of the text—determines perception, initiates development, triggers differentiation of inside and outside.

If this is correct, the hostile attitude towards the other is deeply ingrained and is, so to speak, guaranteed with the construction of the outside world. Xenophobia and hatred of foreigners can easily link up with this primordial tendency.

The projection surfaces and contents can be deconstructed using psychoanalytic conflict psychology. All levels of unconscious emotional conflicts are involved in the formation of prejudice, which is based on the projection of one's own unrecognised aspirations. Some unconscious conflicts, as they are presented by the OPD (2009), can serve as a starting point.

The conflict between individuation and dependence is characterised by threats to demarcation and closeness–distance regulation and is more accurately described by Green as the separation–intrusion dilemma. The more insecure I become in my differentiation from others, in the safeguarding of my boundaries, the more quickly the other becomes an intruder, endangering the integrity of my own person.

The control–submission dynamic describes conflicts that revolve around power and powerlessness or around aggression and its repression. We do not have to go far to find examples of this in Europe or in the USA. Let us take the "Remarks by President Trump during Border Wall Construction", issued on 18 August 2020 by the whitehouse.gov homepage, as an example. In the talk, the acting commissioner Morgan addresses the president of the USA visiting the wall:

> Yes, sir. So, thank you. So first of all, what you see behind me has saved American lives. Every single bit of concrete and steel that goes into the ground, the operational capacity of the men and women you're seeing right here goes exponentially higher to stop dangerous things and people from coming into this country.

Drugs—drugs alone—what this wall does is it helps us shape the behavior of the cartels. It puts us in an offensive position, just like the President said. Because of that, this year—year, to date—we've seized over a million pounds of drugs. Think about that: this year, to date, a million pounds of drugs. And this wall is helping shape the behavior so that we can get better at doing that.

We talked about criminals. We apprehend thousands of criminals every single year. Think about that. You know, a lot of these individuals are violent criminals. Because of this wall, we're able to apprehend and stop these criminals from coming into this country to repeat their offenses. So, we have fewer victims of United States citizens because of the wall, because of what this President has provided us.

Let's talk about gangs. Every single year, we stop hundreds and hundreds of gangs from pouring into this country—like MS-13, whose motto is "Rape, Kill, and Control." That's their motto: "Rape, Kill, and Control." Just recently—it wasn't that long ago—they used machetes to hack up their victims, and they actually leave them decapitated. That's what we're talking about when we're talking about what this tool provides us.

And then, of course, illegal immigration: Even during the height of a global pandemic, illegal immigration continues. And they allow themselves to be put in stash houses that are unsanitary, unsafe. They're put in tractor trailers for days. I mean, there's COVID—that's like a COVID petri dish. But yet, they're coming across. But because of the tools that we have, like this wall, we're able to stop the illegal entry of individuals that have COVID to protect our—a citizen of this country.

(Trump, 20 August 2020)

The words speak for themselves. The wall, according to the commissioner, shelters the honourable US citizen from the Mexicans who bring in danger, drugs, and criminal behaviour; they rape, kill, and control; they even malevolently introduce the "Chinese virus" to the States. (The president underlines in the same talk: "'China plague' is more accurate.") All destructiveness and aggression is projected onto the Mexicans.

Closely connected with the feeling that foreigners take away all achievements, jobs, pension supplies, houses, and yards from "us", the natives, is another preoccupation, namely that they receive more than "us", the natives, that "we" go away empty-handed, but "they" can afford to live in abundance and luxury. This attitude points to the unresolved conflicts concerning the need for care and self-sufficiency. (How much "we" receive because urgently needed skilled workers come to "us" is denied.)

The self-esteem conflict refers to the feelings of superiority or inferiority. Fantasies of sexual grandiosity that are denied are particularly often projected onto members of other cultures and become a stereotype that is charged by oedipal conflicts, for example, when it is about the phantasm of the sexually potent black man or the Thai woman who is always in the mood for love services.

The projection of the sides of the conflict that must not become conscious turns the other into the enemy, the coward, the failure. The projection creates a relationship between the unrecognised own and the construction of the other. The less I know of the foreign and strange parts within myself, the less I will be able to regard the stranger with interest and curiosity. The more I have to fend off what is unknown, unconscious in me, the more I have to fend off what the stranger brings to me.

Self-perception and the image of others belong together and are created simultaneously. Just like the image of the foreign builds the image of one's own identity, we follow Freud in his text on negation, on the unequal distribution of characteristics between the self and the other. Simultaneously with the projection, we must take the opposite mechanism of introjection into account. Projective and introjective processes are interlocking. Identity is not only created by projectively removing what does not fit into the conscious picture from one's own impulses and desires.

At the same time, identity is built at the place of the other. Identity is created through identifications which, as Otto Fenichel (1935) already knew, are internalisations according to an oral mode: the other is "devoured" and appropriated, just as food is assimilated. This applies to the individual characteristic, and to the self-image in general, which comes from the other as a reflection and is appropriated as a mirror image (Lacan, 1949). The finding that the self depends on the other from the outset, that it is interwoven with the other, can be perceived as threatening to identity, and by no means only during puberty. In the course of life, the recognition of this fact can repeatedly become a risk for the idea of one's own autonomy, and therefore there is a danger that the other person will be antagonised just when one might feel dependent on him or her.

The roots of one's own identity in the other are then denied, and the notions of identity freeze, as it were. This applies to personal identity as well as to ethnic identity, in the sense of Mario Erdheim (1992), which regulates "belonging to a tradition of descent" (p. 730), and to cultural identity, which regulates belonging to a culturally determined collective (for differentiation, see Özbek, 2006, p. 98). All three forms of identity—personal, ethnic, and cultural—can harden, especially when they have lost self-evidence and stability for whatever reason. What Dieter Wyss (1973) described for the melancholic, namely that they suffer from "identity sclerosis", applies much more succinctly to the fortress-like, armoured "normal" identity, which leaves no room for flexibility and can thus become extremely dangerous. The German scholar on social psychology Heitmeyer (2010), whose research group has been examining mental reactions to the current socio-cultural-political situation at yearly intervals since 2002, under the title "German Conditions", calls this attitude "Armoured Normality". And this armament belongs to the core inventory of the armouries that prepare for intercultural violence.

The first part can be summarised as follows: psychoanalysis criticises violence by deconstructing the image of the foreigner and examining the projections onto the foreigner. At the same time, it questions the conscious notions of personal identity, or—in terms of a theory of narration—the narratives of one's own self. With the psychoanalytic cure, the static concept of an identity by self-attribution of certain characteristics anchored in consciousness changes into a dynamic or liquefied identity. The static attribution of fixed characteristics of personal identity becomes evident as merely an image of oneself, an imaginary product, which has been formed by one's own life story, by identification with others as role models, but also by the attributions projected on oneself by significant others, as well as by demarcations from others. An image that can be altered and is not immobile. Since it depends on others and is determined by the changing narratives about oneself, identity is not fixed, but "always only a temporary, principally endangered form or structure of the personal self-relationship" (Straub, 2002, p. 263). Identity from a psychoanalytic point of view profits from repeated questioning; identity and non-identity form a productive interplay with each other.

Making boundaries fluid

Thinking from in-between

The image of others and the image of oneself are images, not realities. They are based on the symbolic orders of a group or a society; they do not emerge from nothing, and they attach themselves to guiding cultural ideas and prejudices. Cultural difference is not simply given or predetermined, rather, it is created. Psychoanalysis sets itself the task of resolving hardenings of identity and images of the other, and it can bring this potential into intercultural encounters in order to effectively criticise violence. This is what I wanted to show so far.

But in this critical function *vis-à-vis* established representations of the self and the foreign, the psychoanalytic contribution to the analysis of intercultural violence and the construction of the foreign does not exhaust itself. It can, as it were, begin earlier, not only critically questioning the already completed and established demarcations, but rather leading back before the demarcations and thus observing the representation systems in their dynamics of emergence. Spatial concepts have become firmly established in psychoanalytic theory, with whose help the liquefaction of representations, the worlds of imagination, and the new creations of the intersubjectively anchored imagination are described. In the beginning, there was Winnicott's transitional space (Winnicott, 1953), in which the self-object boundaries are not challenged. This was quickly followed by Lacan's triangular structure of the psyche, whereby the interplay of the real, the imaginary, and the symbolic creates a rift that cannot ever be overcome (Lacan, 1953). Julia Kristeva (1989) has used the image of traversing, of passing through, to mark the affective back and forth between averbal-semiotic and symbolic spaces. Thomas Ogden (1994) has emphasised how in interpersonal work and relatedness a third is created, the analytic third, that is, a creative intersubjective unit that cannot be reduced to the protagonists' proportions. In all these cases (and many others), it is not the one or the other, not the own or the foreign, that is at the beginning, but rather, the transition, the crossing, the third, the crack.

From this point of departure, as already mentioned at the beginning, the "inter" of interculturalism becomes a suffix worth explaining. For it presupposes—otherwise the term makes no linguistic sense—that there is a mediation between the cultures. But if we start from the "between" as that which precedes the variables to be mediated, then we think of the between not as a subsequent connecting link, but as an origin. This "between" is creative, just as Winnicott's transitional space is the starting point for play and Ernst Kris' creativity. The concept of interculturalism is fruitful only when it aims at "interculture" as the basic condition, at the "hybrid" (Bhabha, 1994) as the origin. It is counterproductive when purity or the previously described relationship of identity and difference, of norm and deviation, which tends towards antagonism, are the focus. Instead, the diversity of cultural characteristics that allow for "multiplicity", for multiple forms of life, between which there is freedom of movement, or "accessibility" (Terkessidis, 2010), should be the goal.

It is not for nothing that transcultural psychiatry has discovered the "transcultural transition space" as the space in which it prefers to stay. In transcultural psychotherapy, this space serves as a place for reflection to establish connections of meaning, to locate one's own and the foreign, to relieve feelings of disloyalty and guilt towards the ethnic reference group, and so on. It is a space in which "the different, opposing cultural affiliations and attributions of meaning are present and at the same time are newly created and provided with cultural meaning in the process of understanding" (Machleidt & Gün, 2011, p. 403). And in this sense, the transcultural transitional space unfolds its therapeutic function in the encounter and interaction of the actors, patients, and practitioners. It is ideally located neither inside nor outside, in one's own culture or a foreign culture, and is thus a space in which one's own and the foreign can be "detached and floating" and a common everyday knowledge can be worked out discursively (Özbek & Wohlfart, 2006).

Now this concept, as right as it is, is also in danger of trivialising the circumstances. For this space does not exist as an available entity. It has to be constantly recreated, even in psychotherapy. But not only there. The Indian-American sociologist Homi Bhabha has developed the concept of the "third space". The third space is a space that starts from the in-between, a "threshold space between the determinations of identity"—a space that aims to deconstruct representations and to expose the social or colonial power that lies within them. This third space is certainly related to the "transcultural transitional space". Bhabha's concept, however, has a decisive advantage. From the outset, it reckons with the ruptures that such a space of understanding entails. Bhabha character-ises the third space—in remarkable conceptual agreement with Julia Kristeva—as a "space of continuous crossing" (Bhabha, 1994), in which it is a matter of enduring ambivalence, and of communicating where no understanding can be assumed. In the third space, those processes take place that Jacques Derrida described, in a completely different setting, as risky, "without alibi", without an alternative place. Derrida described and even defined psychoanalysis as an undertaking "without alibi"—an ambiguity that, on closer inspection, is accurate. Without alibi means literally "without another place". Psychoanalysis is not based on eth-ics, on God, or on political convictions, when it comes to grasping the reasons and abysses of the human being or interaction. It allows itself to become involved, on the spot, in the relationship in the here and now, without excuse. Whoever has no alibi has no excuse—he is responsible. As analysts, we cannot analyse unconscious personal and social pro-cesses as if they did not belong to us. The analysis is not carried out in a different place, it is not extraterritorial, the cure is not an appearance of an Habermasian "domination-free space". And yet, a space that—as Derrida himself says—is unconditional, because it does not always and immediately devote itself to the goal of recovery, the goal of restoration, or the like, but allows goals to become visible first of all: entanglement in order to disentangle, aimlessness in order to let goals emerge. In this sense, interculturalism is also risky and without alibi (Derrida, 1990). And yet, the opening-up of the third, transitional space creates an emi-nent chance to prevent violence.

Of course, and this should not be overlooked, the sociological con-cept of the "third space" lacks the conceptual clarity that the reader is looking for. Reading Bhabha's books, on the other hand, promotes cre-ativity and imagination, especially because it does not lead to statistics, but to T. S. Eliot and Joseph Conrad—that is, to literature. Perhaps literature can better show what is meant by a "third space" than a discursive practice. We will therefore, in the third part of this chapter, question a literary text as to whether it can survey the "third space" more precisely and concretely. But before we do so, I will first discuss the task of translation.

The task of translation

In the transitional space, representations emerge, terms are created, or they are examined for their meaning, which varies from one language to another. This is exactly the task of the translator. Psychoanalysis as a therapy in a broad sense is also always concerned with the translation of meanings: what does the analyst want to tell me via his words and verbal associations, what does the symptom convey as message? The problem of translation arises in every psychoanalytic session.

Psychoanalysis can bring this expertise to intercultural work in the "third space". Interculturalism requires translation. This is not new. Four phases in the history of intercultural translation theories have previously been distinguished (see Schahadat, 2013):

The first phase was concerned with the question of how texts are to be translated from one language into another.

The second phase was characterised by the deconstruction of the translation as a necessary failure; the translator is indebted to the text because of the lack of original reproduction. He or she pays this debt by trying to retain the meaning of the text, and at the same time guarantees the survival of the original in the translation.

The third phase goes hand in hand with the cultural turn in the field of translation, which is changing from the translation of languages to the translation of cultures. "In fact, translation is increasingly detached from the linguistic-textual paradigm and recognized as an indispensable practice in a world of interdependence and interconnectedness" (Bachmann-Medick, 2006, p. 176). The anthropologist Talal Asad, who grew up in India, Pakistan, and England, has explicitly described the translation of cultures as a psychoanalytic act (cf. Schahadat, 2013, p. 35).

The fourth phase is characterised by the translational turn, in which the concept of translation itself becomes a paradigm for other fields as well, that is, it expands. This fourth phase is characterised by a transdisciplinary approach.

What does psychoanalysis have to add to the problem of translation? Psychoanalysis as the art of translation participates in all phases, but it adds something to each phase. So it is no coincidence that it has been taken up by all theories of translation. Different dimensions of psychoanalytic translation are summarised now:

Psychoanalytic translation is initially directed at the "exchange of words" described by Freud as the essence of psychoanalysis. However, there is no authorial translator in the cure; the correctness of the translation given in an interpretation is proven only in the process of psychoanalysis and the shared therapeutic practice, for example, in the spreading of associations made possible by an interpretation, and the resulting expansion of the analysand's scope of thoughts and action. In the psychoanalytic transitional space, as in the third space of interculturality, there is no meta-language that monitors the correctness or incorrectness of the translations.

What is being translated, however, is not a text that only one of the partners in the analysis delivers. Rather, it is a text that is engendered by the analytical dialogue, by the unconscious scenes evolving in analysis, by all participants, and this is comparable to that which the cultural turn emphasises. There is no such thing as a text that the one produces alone and the other has only to interpret. Rather, both elaborate the text, which they must then understand together. It is precisely this model that can be important for intercultural practice.

Psychoanalytic work therefore always has to do with self-reflection and self-criticism, which takes the flawed nature of every translation into account, as much as the violence that can lie in the translation itself. This is the purpose of countertransference analysis. As an analyst, I reflect on the part I play in the creation of the common text. As an analyst, I also know that my interpretive activity is a translation that necessarily changes the text to be translated. In psychoanalysis—and this aspect can also be profitably extended to transcultural practice— translation always proves to be a performative practice (Wagner, 2012), which influences the element to be translated by transforming it into another horizon of meaning.

Nevertheless, psychoanalytic translation proceeds even further, when the additional effect becomes clear through the comparison of psychopathological and psychoanalytic work on the symptom. In psychopathology, the symptom is described, maybe even translated, that is, transferred into other contexts of meaning, but only in psychoanalysis is the symptom itself understood as a translation. The task of treatment is to reconstruct the absent text, the translation of which is the symptom.

In psychoanalysis, the object of translation thus expands, starting off with the words and the behaviour of the analysand and finally addressing fantasies and jointly created and staged interactional scenes. The implicit translational activity that leads to the emergence of a symptom—a translational activity of the subject—is appreciated even where it is not understood as a subjective intention at all. Only via transitional spaces as methodological prerequisites it is possible to translate properly. In other words, transitional spaces are created by the psychoanalytic setting and its basic principles. These include the form of listening that renounces the violence of hasty presuppositions of meaning, the way of expanding the field of observation and of conceiving the other, as well as oneself, as part and origin of this field, and the way of conceiving contributions of the other not only as material, but as interpretation of interpersonal stagings.

Tracks

Third spaces, in which such broad translation activity is possible, protect from violence and criticise violence, even if they are about violence. Literary texts, if they succeed, make such spaces available to the reader; literature is not only translated, it can also translate itself, even in intercultural contexts. A "translating text" (Bandia, 2006) is a text that contains translations in itself *before* its linguistic translation, both in the concrete and the figurative sense (cf. Wagner, 2012, p. 40). In my opinion, the novel *Tracks* by the author Louise Erdrich is a particularly worthwhile example of a translating text. As a literary text, it opens up a third space in which intercultural violence, to which the novel bears witness throughout, is abolished, that is, preserved and transcended in its presentation.

Since Louise Erdrich has remained largely unknown to European readers, despite her numerous awards in the USA, and although many of her works have been translated and published, a few words about her biography might be useful, because it shows how anchored her own life is in intercultural fields of tension. Erdrich was born in Minnesota, USA. Her father is from Germany, and her mother has French roots on her paternal side. Her maternal grandfather was a long-time tribal leader of the Turtle Mountain Band of Chippewa Indians from the Ojibwe or Anishinabe tribe—the fourth-largest Native American Indian group, of whom today about 60,000 live in the USA between Michigan and Montana, and about 80,000 in Canada.

The novel *Tracks* is set in the 1920s in the Anishinabe community in North Dakota. The structure of the text is complex and artful, and already shows by its very structure that there is not one, authorial narrator, but rather two. The unbiased, uninformed reader needs time to come to terms with the characters and storylines in the book, since a summary feigns an order that does not exist. The reader is dependent on a "bricolage", on assembling the identities of the main characters. This is what constitutes the formal quality of the text: the reader first has to find the persons in the reading, then invent and construct. But the reader never fully finds the characters—only as the focus of different narrative perspectives, to which the reader necessarily adds their own understanding.

Nanapush, a narrator, tells his granddaughter Lulu retrospectively about the events of the years 1912 to 1924. Lulu has a right, Nanapush thinks, to know why her mother, his daughter Fleur, sent her away at the age of ten so that the child had to grow up without her mother. Fleur, as we readers learn at some point, is not the biological daughter of Nanapush at all. When an epidemic raged on the Indian reservation, he saved her from death, which brings them together and gives him the right to define her as a daughter.

Fleur, we learn little by little, has left the reserve to work in the fictitious city of Argus, where she continuously wins poker games against male players, strangely enough, exactly one dollar every evening. One evening, she earns excessive money and is raped by her male game opponents on the same night. The following day, we hear later, the city is hit by a tornado. Only the rapists perish, and their bodies are later found in the refrigerator of a butcher where they had taken refuge.

Fleur returns to the reservation and meets Eli, who falls in love with her and moves in with her. She is pregnant, but it remains unclear whether as a result of the rape. In any case, Eli takes on the paternity of the child, Lulu. Fleur anchors herself again in her Indian culture after she returns from the city, but she lives on the edge, isolated. The text attributes mystical abilities to her, and she expresses eroticism and power in her personal accounts, and many legends are dedicated to her.

Pauline is the second narrator from whose perspective we reconstruct the plot. Unlike Fleur, she wants to get rid of the Indian culture that has shaped her by any possible means. She refuses to speak the language of the Anishinabe. She goes to a Christian monastery and tortures herself with cruel self-flagellation until she hears the voice of Jesus, who absolves her from her origin. She then tries to convert the tribe members to the Christian faith—especially Fleur—and also learns nursing from a widow.

Even if Fleur and Pauline are far apart from each other in terms of the novel's construction, because Pauline is the narrator and Fleur is the heroine of the novel, they are related to each other in terms of content, like two opposites: Fleur, it seems, fights against any form of assimilation, as shown by her fierce defence of Indian identity, while Pauline urgently wants to get rid of hers. Both fail in an identity construction that either does not allow development at all, or only under unspeakable suffering. And both live out the suppressed cultural other, Fleur by first earning money in the city and playing cards, Pauline by using magic to destroy Fleur, of whom she is jealous: she uses a love spell to inflame Eli, Fleur's partner, for another woman. Fleur is a projective screen for Pauline, who projects the denied sensual and wild sides of her own identity onto her, so that Fleur becomes a distorted image of the wild natives.

Fleur and Pauline also have something in common: they both use violence, but each in a completely different form. Fleur provokes, uses magical abilities against others, and has probably killed her rapists. When she hears that Nanapush's partner was attacked and scalped, she takes revenge without hesitation. Pauline is more indirectly violent, but on the other hand, more cruel. She observes Fleur's rape without intervening in any way. She also directs violence against herself and fights the projected evil not only in others, but also on her own body. She does not translate, but repeats, and thus the novel points to an important dynamic in the perpetuation of transcultural violence, including all forms of traumatic violence. The aggression to which the victim of cultural violence is exposed does not disappear or vanish into thin air—a fact that is very often overlooked in trauma therapy. Rather, the violence suffered is internalised by becoming part of the victim's own identity and leads to the victim becoming violent as well. This is what Pauline stands for.

Back to Nanapush, the most interesting figure for our context. The reader learns much from him as a narrator, but the reader must also realise that Nanapush is lying, that they cannot expect to learn the truth. But Nanapush lies with good intention, and he has a sense of humour. His character is conceived after the model of the trickster, the rogue, who plays an important role in Indian literature. Karl Kerényi and C. G. Jung built a monument to this figure in the 1954 book *The Divine Prankster* (Radin, Kerényi, & Jung, 1954)—but also a highly problematic one. In any case, the definition C. G. Jung gives exposes his own intercultural arrogance. For in Jung's case, even the trickster is striving for a "higher consciousness".

> The trickster is a primitive "cosmic" being of divine-animal nature, on the one hand superior to man because of his superhuman qualities, and on the other hand inferior to him because of his unreason and unconsciousness. He is no match for the animals either, because of his extraordinary clumsiness and lack of instinct. These defects are the marks of his human nature, which is not so well adapted to the environment as the animal's but, instead, has prospects of a much higher development of consciousness based on a considerable eagerness to learn, as is duly emphasized in the myth.
>
> (Jung & Read, 1968, p. 254)

So even the trickster, the prankster, has his eyes set on further and higher development. The following description, which Hynes gave, seems much more appropriate: "The sheer wealth of trickster phenomena can easily lead one to believe that the trickster is indefinable. To define means to draw boundaries, and Tricksters seem to be surprisingly resistant to limitations. They are compulsive border crossers" (Hynes, 1993, p. 33).

In this reading, Nanapush, the trickster of the novel, embodies the one who is most likely to be able to use the third spaces with his transgressions of borders. He remains rooted in his ethnic identity, and yet he faces historical and violent changes, and reckons with them without denying them, also without giving up his humour and ridicule.

The seemingly casual remark that Nanapush was the official translator (Erdrich, 1988, p. 127) fits in with this. He mediates, even with the hated white exploiters and speculators whose character he very well recognises. He negotiates, tied up and lying powerlessly on the ground, with the white people who overpower his partner, and thus succeeds in preventing them from killing the partner, only scalping her. This is how he gets through, without illusions, but with an unbroken love of life. He does not let his sense of lust be taken away and immediately erotically cathexes the bald head of his partner. But he doesn't forget his plans of revenge, and elatedly sets traps for the perpetrators—concrete traps in which they are caught.

The fascination of the novel lies in the fact that the third space does not appear in the described plot and content of the novel, which is largely about the destruction of an Indian culture, but instead in the formal design and language itself. It is language, and Nanapush as its carrier, that spans the third space. Without a doubt, the novel is written in English, the language of the victorious English-American white culture. The "old language" does not appear anywhere, except in a few names. And the name has power:

> My dear child, listen carefully. Nanapush is a name that loses its power as often as it is written down and recorded in an official file. That's why I only mentioned it once in all these years … I could have written my name, and a lot more, in engraved writing. I was educated by the Jesuits in the halls of St. John before I ran back into the woods and forgot all my prayers. My father said: "Nanapush: that is what they will call you. Because the name has to do with cunning and with life in the bush. Because

it has to do with something that girls can't resist. The first Nanapush stole fire, you will steal hearts."

(p. 46f)

In the last sentence, the trickster Nanapush is placed in close proximity
to the Greek trickster Prometheus, who is punished by the gods because
he does not accept the boundaries between heaven and earth, and steals
fire from the gods. But it is not only the name that is guarded cunningly
in a world that robs the name of its radiance. In the third room, as it
were, the experiences of transition romp about, the reports of both nar-
rators change from the magical to the sober, from the traditional to the
destroyed, from violence to revenge, without any arising contradiction.
Nanapush's agility is convincing because it is used playfully; from it
arises the spark that gives hope, because in the midst of all violence and
without denial, a hybrid identity is lived.

Nanapush reports: "Later, when I approached Fleur's hut, the trees
were still untouched in their monotony, so high, so cool." It is worth
noting that, in the original English version, it says: "the woods were
still untouched in sameness, so high, so cool" (Erdrich, 1988, p. 209).
It is not monotony, but self-sufficiency, that distinguishes the woods.
Nevertheless, the German text continues: "The wind in their branches
was an airy canopy. I did not know why I had ever been afraid of them,
why I had ever wished to interpret the language of the foliage." In the
English text, it sounds different again: "why I ever wished to translate
the language of their leaves". No, it is not about interpretation, but really
about translation, which is not necessary when man and nature are
connected. "The path became narrower again, and I felt my ghostly relatives coming closer, felt the rustling of their airy thoughts and laments.
I was completely engrossed in my thoughts when a little wild girl with
branches in her hair attacked me, held me by the legs and searched my
pockets for a mint" (Erdrich, 1988, p. 257).

The airy spirits and Lulu's firm gesture naturally have their place
next to each other.

Finally, and above all, the destroyed traditions are preserved in the
very sensual, dense, pictorial language, which is free of false pathos and
can very quickly become saturated with coarseness. The following passage is about how Nanapush warms his granddaughter and saves her

from freezing to death after he refused to amputate Lulu's frozen leg, having refused the help of European medicine:

> Many times in my life, during the time my children were born, I have wondered what it is like to be a woman and to be able to create a human being from the additional substances of her own body. In the terrible times, in the calamity I don't want to talk about, when the earth took again (swallowed back in the original) what it had given me to love, I gave birth to loss. I was like a woman in my suffering, but my children were all delivered to death. It was the opposite, but now I had the opportunity to put things in the right order.
>
> Finally my songs overcame the painful burning. You were in uncertainty, and your eyes were open and looked into mine. Once I had you again, I didn't dare to let the wire between us break off and moved my lips further and further, keeping you still with my talking, just like now. For the first time in my life, it was my duty, but also my joy, to hold out all night and far into the next morning.
>
> (p. 206)

In this short passage, Nanapush's figure is once again placed in intertextual proximity to the Occidental-Western tradition, in that his intersexual quality is all too clearly reminiscent of the Greek visionary Tiresias, the only person according to Greek mythology who knows what it is like to have experiences both as a woman and as a man. At the same time, in the intensity of the choice of images, through which death and life, but also the life-supporting power of language, are depicted in condensed form, the lost Indian culture comes alive "when the earth took back what it had given me to love", or "I did not dare to let the wire between us break off and moved my lips further and further, kept you still with my talking, just like now" (p. 206).

In the English language, which cannot be seen but as a language of violence against the native culture in the USA, another language is suspended—it sounds in the images that vanish just as quickly again to give way to reality, which is now anything but tender and imaginative.

Rather, it is about cutting down trees and selling land, about rape and murder. Once again: "keep still with my talking, just like now". This is what Nanapush manages to do, as he describes confidently. This is what the author accomplishes—to make the reader keep still in a fascinated way, in the face of a reading that never causes depression, even if it is about violence and destruction.

Thus, the book lives from a radical hope. Psychoanalysis-prone philosopher Jonathan Lear published a book of the same name, *Radical Hope* (2006), in which he describes the downfall of the Crowe Indian tribe. Radical hope is linked to a dream of the last Crowe chief, Plenty Coups, and the cultural tradition of this dream as a preserving narrative. The hope unfolded by Louise Erdrich is even more radical because it appears nowhere else but in the literary language, which is capable of making reading a sensual pleasure and thus hopeful. Affect and passion, magical visual power, and psychological clarity—they all meet in a condensed form in the poetic transitional space of the novel's words. The transitional space is allegorised in the person of Nanapush as the trickster, and the person of Nanapush lives in speech and language. The traces, tracks, of the novel, which are indicated in the title, thus ultimately lead to language, and this is precisely where hope lies, because, as Walter Benjamin described, it is language that is "a sphere of human agreement that is non-violent to the extent that it is wholly inaccessible to violence: the proper sphere of 'understanding'" (W. Benjamin, 1921, p. 245).

Tracks is thus a translating text in several respects: it translates the native language of the Indian culture into English, whereby this language is conjured up only by means of a few names—otherwise, it does not exist anywhere in the original, but only in this translation. Secondly, it translates the thinking of an oppressed culture into the thinking of the oppressing culture. Thirdly, it makes it clear in its form that the members, especially women, of a violently oppressed culture can only be revived in traces, never completely, never uniformly. And fourthly, it makes it clear at the same time that the translation profits from the original language, which cannot be found undamaged anywhere, as it is poetically alive and creates new living spaces.

CHAPTER 6

Dying in literature and psychoanalysis— *Everyman* (P. Roth)

The necessity to die is not limited to old age, but with increasing age it draws more and more clearly and unstoppably nearer. Dying provokes fear, but it still needs clarifying why this is, although the question has occupied philosophy at least since Plato's dialogue *The Symposium*. In the German language, the word *Tod* (death) entails an equivocation: we speak of death as the final result, but also of death as a process of dying. The state of being dead cannot cause fear, for the subject who could have felt the fear no longer exists. Fear therefore refers exclusively to the transition, to dying. Therefore, fear of death is fear of dying.

Even death, or better, our idea of death, is subject to historical transformations. In the early Middle Ages, death was thought to derive from divine providence, whether as punishment or redemption. Only towards the end of the Middle Ages is it presented as an independent power that stands above even the angels and the devils (Illich, 1992). This is how the Dances of the Dead, the *danses macabres*, are created, which show in pictorially comprehensible form that death reaches everyone, without regard to merit or honour, similar to the mystery plays of *Jedermann* (Everyman).

At the same time, theologians wrote guidebooks on how man should prepare himself for dying; the *"ars moriendi"* was newly taught and cultivated. The sermon by the young Martin Luther which was entitled "From Preparation to Dying", written in 1519 (Koch, 2011), is still well known today. To speak of the "art of dying" today sounds clumsy, and it is not without reason that the phrase "art of living" is much more familiar to us. Terminal care is not to be equated with the art of dying. Terminal care and support in dying are limited to the activities of priests and theologians and to the duties of doctors and psychotherapists, while the art of dying should include instructions for everyone, including priests and helpers. But who teaches the art of dying today in a secular age (Taylor, 2007), and who teaches the companions in the dying process how one could die properly? They have no own practice in this, obviously, because dying is characterised by its unreplaceable uniqueness. Dying cannot be learned from personal experience. One's own death is not a fact of experience, but only a future event that is certain to occur—a "premonition of an incomprehensible kind" (Fink, 1992, p. 149). When death occurs, it destroys the subject who could experience it. Dying heralds "an experience of which the subject is not master" (Levinas, 1984, p. 43). In principle, death can only be experienced indirectly, as the death of others, or the death of the stranger. Hence the great interest in forms of experience close to death, which is also the subject of current research projects (Bühler & Peng-Keller, 2014), in order to learn something about dying itself from the experiences we hear from others.

How and where else can you learn the *ars moriendi*? Can literature take over the task? What help can psychoanalysis offer? The question can be narrowed down further: what are the life-historical—and I emphasise: *life-historical*—tasks in preparation for dying that psychoanalysis can illuminate? What answers does literature give, what ways does it guide to the solution of these tasks? This is the simple structure of the following explanations. First, the retroactive nature of dying onto the life process or on one's own life story must be characterised. Psychoanalytical and philosophical thoughts are used like a quarry, without regard to their infinitely ramified theoretical contexts. Afterwards, I will not deal with literature in general, but will compare and interpret two literary texts, namely two versions of the Everyman theme: the play with the same name, *Jedermann*, by Hugo von Hofmannsthal that is still presented each year at the Salzburg Summer Festival, and Philip Roth's novel *Everyman*.

Dying as a challenge for the life story

As we said initially, dying is an inevitable and ubiquitous fact. Nevertheless, human experience refuses to acknowledge it.

> Of course I know that I myself must die. Of course I also know that the end is coming closer and closer to me, I prepare myself for it, make practical preparations. Of course I know for certain that I will die, that I will be no more. But it is strange: if I pay close attention to it—in secret I do not believe in it.
>
> (Sternberger, 1981, p. 30)

This statement by the political scientist and philosopher Dolf Sternberger, who wrote the haunting "Petites Perceptions" on death, can be easily combined with Freud's statement that the unconscious does not know death (Freud, 1915b, p. 289). For Freud, Sternberger's "in secret" is the corollary of desire. One's own desires, which always aim at fulfilment, that is, are oriented towards the future, prevail over the knowledge of finiteness. The experience of death is beyond the pleasure principle. The first challenge of dying, thus, is to cope with the dilemma of rational knowledge and desire, of repression and recognition of mortality. It focuses on the relationship between drive and transience.

Perhaps it is not so much the unwillingness as the impossibility to represent death itself, despite all allegorical or pictorial representations. For death cannot be grasped; it stands for the crack that does not heal in life. It is not negotiable, not representable, not embeddable in a meaning that can be represented or thought (B.-C. Han, 1998). It deconstructs the self-interpretation and the personal narrative of oneself and one's own life that everyone is ready to present and through which human identity is constituted. Thus, something which cannot be represented belongs to life as its limit. A limit, however, can only be perceived when it is transcended. In one's own experience, death has no afterlife. The narrative that one gives of oneself, in order to represent the personal life, ends with death. No, it stops before death; the story of one's own life cannot, in principle, be concluded. It cannot be told completely, if the very last moments of dying are counted as part of life.

In dying, then, there is a "beyond narrative", and all *ars moriendi* aims to anticipate what can no longer be told. Narrating, as the literary scholar Volker Klotz states, is *"enttöten"*, a made-up word in German, a "de-killing" (Klotz, 2006, p. 233), and narrating as a process "opposes the senseless lethal loss through meaningful production" (ibid.). The second challenge of dying that life faces is thus to respond to the end of the narrative only by means of a narration. The unrepresentable cannot be represented, but we cannot refrain from trying to do so. It touches on the experience of negativity, lack, and processing them with the help of the only things available: the world of signs or symbols.

A narrative is directed towards the future because it lives from a temporal sequence that is most directly expressed in children's stories: "And then … and then … and then … and then." Narratives progress in time. Dying is the end of the narrative I can give of myself and marks the end of my own orientation towards the future. One's own death exists only in the future, at most in the present moment of dying—although it is unclear how much of it enters into the consciousness that just disappears in dying. But under no circumstances does it exist in the past, if belief in the afterlife is excluded. To be present, and to project oneself in the present moment towards what is coming, and to mobilise and animate past experiences for what is important at the moment, that characterises human experience from a temporal perspective. This temporality of experience vanishes during dying.

For the others who mourn the dead, there is a before and an after; they can build the death of the other into their own personal life according to the temporality of the experience. This is not so for the dying person. But to imagine a future without one's own person is obviously contrary to the egocentricity of one's own experience. In other words, one's own narcissism does not allow the future to be left unimagined. Age, however, becomes a "period of life in which the future is reduced" (Marquard, 2013, p. 80). With it, as the philosopher Odo Marquard also precisely states, the illusion of completion is lost: "our death is stronger than our goals" (p. 71). The third challenge posed by dying on life, then, is to cope with this dilemma between the inescapable focus on goals, that is, on the future, and the increasing reduction of the future.

It violates narcissism, which is directed towards the eternity of one's own presence on earth.

Reference to the narcissistic mortification by the certainty of one's own death names a further challenge of dying. *"Non omnis confundar"*: the philosopher of hope, Ernst Bloch (1986), has highlighted the utopian grip on the imperishable in the musical motifs of Brahms' *Requiem* or the late Schubert string quartets. All the regulations and decrees that most people make for the time after their death bear witness to this concern, even if only in their wills. Something should remain of me and survive. Sternberger has repeatedly pointed out that living on after death is only possible in the memory of others. When it is lost, everything is over. Trust in the future, which is no longer one's own but that of others, requires that a distinction be made between life time and world time (Blumenberg, 1986): the world does not end with one's own death—some things I do only benefit descendants (Scheffler, 2013). This thought, which is admittedly difficult to think, might reduce the fear of dying, at least that is what the philosopher Ernst Tugendhat convincingly demonstrates. According to him, we fear death because we lack serenity, we cannot let go or desist. We cannot avoid taking ourselves seriously and thinking that we ourselves are the theatre that is life. "Death and already aging contain the chance to realize this error and to step to the side within the theater, so to speak, and leave the center" (Tugendhat, 2006, p. 51). The fourth challenge can be summarised as the conflict between centring and decentring in the perspective of life. It belongs, as already mentioned, to the narcissistic provocations of dying.

Finally, the phrase *"non omnis confundar"* raises the question concerning the others. Death confronts people with a fathomless loneliness. In the run-up to death, existential philosophy sees the fundamental experience of existence, of the personal, individual being that can only be accounted for personally. One must die alone. In the words of Martin Heidegger: "The non-relational character of death, as understood in anticipation, individualizes existence down to itself" (Heidegger, 1962, p. 308). The reference to others is lost in the moment of dying. And yet the others play an important role in two respects. Are they present, do they support the dying person, even if they cannot spare or relieve them of death? And have the relational experiences during the lifetime been strong enough to create a basic trust? This is what psychoanalytical object-relationship psychology can offer concerning the imminent process of dying by activating the bonds or good inner objects that can facilitate the experience of death. This last challenge can be described as the dilemma between the radical loneliness in dying and the relationship to others.

In the second part, we will now look at how the challenges described above are met in two literary works that—almost a century apart—depict dying itself.

Dying in literature: *Jedermann*

Jedermann

Hugo von Hofmannsthal published his play *Everyman: The Play of the Rich Man's Death* (*Jedermann. Das Spiel vom Sterben des reichen Mannes*) in 1911. To this day, it is performed annually during the Salzburg Festival, in good weather at the Cathedral Square. That is where it belongs: it begins with the voice of God, which, depending on the production, often resounds from the cathedral towers. God calls upon his messenger, Death, to go to Everyman. Death reaches him in the middle of life. Everyman, the rich man, is hard towards a debtor, inattentive towards his mother, erotically inflamed towards his girlfriend, who is called Buhlschaft (Paramour) in the play. He is surrounded by flatterers, the Friend first, then the Fat and the Thin Cousin.

Death reaches for him during a banquet—the death bells are inaudible to bystanders, as is the call for Everyman that he alone can hear, which in Salzburg emanates from the battlements of the fortress and from other places near and far onto the Cathedral Square. Now Everyman is looking for support, for people to accompany him on his last journey, but he does not find any, they all elude his, the dying man's, call. In his mortal fear, he falls back on his wealth, wants to subdue Mammon, the personification of money, to accompany him, but Mammon makes it clear to him who is great and who is small. Left alone, Everyman receives an offer of support only by Good Deeds, a weak woman who embodies the little good that Everyman has accomplished during his life. She calls a stronger person, Faith, to help. Everyman repents; Faith and Works, now strengthened, support him in his descent into the grave, where, in the end, the Devil, who was sure of Everyman's soul, must abdicate.

The first challenge of dying, as we have seen, can be described as the dilemma of rational knowledge and desire—of repression and recognition of mortality. Hofmannsthal dramatically stages this struggle. It most impressively appears condensed in a clash of contradictory terms: Everyman voices an introductory toast in the beginning of his lustful banquet, as he is sitting side by side with his Friend, and is greeting his guests: "You are all very welcome, Do me the last honour today!" In this phrase, lust and death suddenly collide. In the course of the play, the spectators become witnesses of how the repression and the proximity of death struggle with each other in Everyman.

The second challenge was to represent the unrepresentable having to capture experiences of negativity and lack with the help of an incomplete, inadequate repertoire of signs. Hofmannsthal's play, which continues the tradition of late medieval mystery plays, has an easy time in this respect at first, it seems, because it can use personifications for the representation of experiences. Death and Devil have their personal appearances. Near the end, new, hitherto unknown representations emerge: the Good Works and Faith. However negative the end of life may appear, in the play, it is turned into a conciliatory ending, according to the Christian tradition, in which the play literally inscribes itself from the first word, which is the Word of God. The negativity of dying then is only transition, the despair that Everyman feels does prepare for conversion and salvation. In the face of death, the scope of what Everyman can envisage and think about himself expands. The negativity of dying leads to purification. Perhaps this transfiguring and positive view of dying is the core of the unwavering popularity that accompanies the Everyman in the Salzburg Festival and elsewhere.

The third challenge posed by dying for the living is to cope with the dilemma between the inevitable focus on goals, that is, on the future, and the increasing reduction of future perspectives. Again, personifications or allegories facilitate the staging of this dilemma best and most clearly in the dialogue between Everyman and Mammon. His money had been used to open all doors, and to implement all plans. But Mammon resists facing the last step, making it clear to Everyman that it is no longer him that has the power: Everyman has not had the money, rather, the money/Mammon has had him in his hand.

The fourth challenge is summarised as a conflict between centring and decentring in perspectives on life. The play does not meet this challenge. Supported by faith—Faith as a person—Everyman struggles for a change in his understanding of God, in order to arrive at a different approach that encompasses God as not only the master of power and punishment, but also the God of grace and forgiveness. In this struggle, he remains completely self-centred until the last moment, in which he descends step by step into the grave. No other is allowed into his last thoughts; only he, in his relationship with God, remains the object of his thoughts. Then the play ends. There is no "beyond narcissism", which makes the conversion and purification of Everyman ultimately unbelievable, lest one assumes an intention and secret self-criticism of the author. Everyman does not step back, he does not really turn around; in the way he repents and changes his morality, Everyman remains as egomaniacal as he has been before.

This leads to the final challenge—the dilemma between the radical loneliness in dying and the reference to others. The text impressively demonstrates how a person is left alone when dying: no journeyman, no relative, no lover wants to go down this last path. On the other hand, Everyman is not alone. The personified values step in as replacements for human beings, to which Everyman opens up in his conversion, and these are Christian values. His walking stick into the hereafter is held by Faith and Works. It is not precisely representations of experience, but rather, the recourse to newly created values founded in religion that help on the path to death. The reference to others becomes unnecessary—to believe, then, means no longer having to refer to other people, because the values connect with God. This is the privilege of religion, which in this sense negates dying itself: "Death, where is your sting?" Bad luck exists only for those who do not follow this Christian path.

Everyman

Almost a century later, in Philip Roth's novel *Everyman*, published in 2005 as one of the author's last texts (short novels), alongside *Nemesis* (2010), *The Humbling* (2009), and *Indignation* (2008), we encounter Everyman in a completely different context. Everyman does not live in a Christian society, but—as almost always with Philip Roth—in a Jewish community in New Jersey, although Judaism appears only in the funeral rites and nowhere else explicitly. The voice of God does not chime at the beginning, instead the novel starts with the three words "around the grave". It begins with Everyman's funeral, and he is introduced in the reflections given by his few surviving relatives. His daughter Nancy gives a short eulogy in which she cites her father by mentioning what Everyman had been given as a fatherly maxim, and this principle is put into pervasive practice in the book: "You cannot change reality. One must take it as it comes" (p. 5). Everyman's reality in the novel is death, and rather than denying it, the text introduces it from the very beginning. The paternal maxim applies—this is a trick of the novel—not only to the protagonist and his way of life, but also very much to the mode of representation chosen by the author. It is unsparing.

In a lengthy second eulogy, his elder brother Howie, the other important figure in Everyman's life, a person who has been frighteningly healthy and successful, tells us that Everyman is the son of a jeweller and watchmaker. His father used him as a courier for the delivery of diamonds. Diamonds are notable for being resistant to time. On the other hand, the young Everyman's passion centres on his father's watches—he listens to them ticking, "if they still did. That's what made that boy tick." Everyman ticks—he lives in and through time. This text is stretched out from the first pages between the incessantly advancing ticking of the clock, and that which should remain timeless.

Everyman reveals just how badly he deals with what lasts in a small episode, namely when he gives a diamond to his third wife Merete—his least sustainable and therefore most short-lived romantic relationship—and quotes his father: "Apart from beauty and prestige and value, the diamond is imperishable." Everyman doesn't simply give it to her as a present. He pushes it between her teeth to let her suck on it. Like Hofmannsthal's character Paramour, Merete is not able to accompany Everyman during his time of suffering: Everyman uses the diamond as a symbol of immortality to increase his lust and desire—he can't help it. Immediately afterwards, death intervenes, not yet his death at this point, but the death of his mother. Later, the text presents a touching, fleeting encounter between the aged Everyman and a jogger. He speaks to her, sexually fascinated by the young woman, and asks her, "How game are you?" (p. 132). She reacts in a friendly way, he gives her his phone number, but she will never call. Until the end, eroticism fights against decay in Everyman, which is how Roth deals with what was described as the first challenge.

And decay is presented mercilessly. The novel has the form of a rondo: it begins with the funeral, then devotes itself to several episodes of Everyman's life, only to return to his last breaths at the end. In allowing Everyman's life to pass by in small vivid miniatures, the central part, however, shows no unity, which is reflected in the development and identity formation of the protagonist's personality, especially in his casually mentioned professional successes or his experiences in relationships. The novel discloses the need to narrate—to give direction to one's own life—as an illusion through its finely woven structure, thus finding an answer to our second challenge. There is indeed a thread that holds the life story together; but unlike in classical or even modern development novels, it is nothing else but the medical dossier that continually swells with age that is the uniting red thread. Thus, the chronology of Everyman's life story is structured according to the increasingly dense episodes of illness. The statement "Age is not a struggle; old age is a massacre" (p. 156) is the brutal quintessence of the process of decay that structures life. Everyman's basic conviction, his "philosophical niche" fits the bill: "If he ever wrote an autobiography, it would be called: life and death of a male body." Again and again, very small autobiographical summaries insert themselves into the text—reflections that Everyman directs to his own life. They don't show a heroic story, but rather a failure: "Well, he was divorced three times, a former serial spouse whose devotion was no less than his misdeeds and mistakes" (p. 156). But this does not mean that Everyman dies in a contrite way. In the end, before his last operation, from which he will not wake up, he enjoys the sunlight: "he sank down, but felt anything but defeated, not doomed at all, only eager to experience fulfillment again, and yet he never woke up" (p. 182). After that, only three sentences follow: "Cardiac arrest. He was no more, freed from being, entering into nowhere without even knowing it. Just as he'd feared from the start." For Roth's Everyman, there is no redemption, no solution, neither in a salutary or a destructive direction, therefore there is neither heaven nor continuous despair, only the constant tossing back and forth between the experience of nothingness and narrative—our second challenge which dying poses to life.

The perspective of ageing as a massacre also affects one's interests and newly developed fields of activity after retirement. (Of course, in this respect, the protagonist is really everyone, because who is not moved by the prospect of being able to devote themselves to other things after a bread-and-butter job?) First it is reading, then the former advertising specialist discovers a new talent for painting; he gives painting lessons, gains recognition in the retirement home to which he had moved, and is successful. But in view of the progressive ageing process, he soon can see no more sense in painting; characteristically, he tells his daughter, who wants to preserve his intentions, that he has had an "irreversible aesthetic vasectomy" (p. 103). He sees painting as a way of exorcising old age: "Suddenly he floated in nothingness, in the sound of the syllable 'nothing' and in nothingness, and terrible fear spread" (p. 103). It is difficult for him to occupy his own future, beyond living towards death. He always fails anew, confronted with what we listed as the third challenge.

The fourth challenge described the dilemma between centring and decentring one's own life. Even Everyman cannot leave the stage; he remains in its centre and does not step aside. However, there are a few touching moments when he succeeds in decentring, even for a brief moment. In a beautiful intertextual allusion to *Hamlet*, he encounters the gravedigger as he goes to the Jewish cemetery, which the reader knows from the very beginning as his burial site. He talks to the gravedigger in a way that no one else has ever talked to him: he is empathic, he inquires in detail about the techniques the gravedigger uses, asks him whether he buried his father as well, and for a brief moment, he foresees that he himself will be buried by the same man. Such passages in the text are rare; however, whereas Everyman can achieve a decentration only in small, specially tuned moments, the author constantly demonstrates his decentration to the reader. For he never lets Everyman become a first-person narrator, even when portraying his own fantasies. Occasionally, direct and distanced reference is made to his Everyman status: "As always—and like almost everyone else—he did not want to have to experience the end a moment earlier than was absolutely necessary" (p. 66). This is what makes the book a hard read: the reader is invited to participate in a fate, but he is never allowed to rest in identification with the protagonist. Through formal decentration, we are inevitably confronted with the fact that the text is negotiating with us. But this does not mean that we will not be able to adjust to the hero in the next moment. Here too, the reader is not released from the strict ambivalence towards the dilemmas of dying.

The fifth challenge is the dilemma between relatedness and the loneliness in dying. In *Everyman*, the agony of age-related loneliness clearly predominates. With each surgical operation, one person who could have accompanied Everyman falls away. Suffering from diseases which increasingly turn into "sicknesses unto death" (Kierkegaard) is doubled by the gradually increasing loneliness. Either people fall away or literally fall over, like the aforementioned erotic playmate Merete, who is constitutionally incapable of suffering but also terribly impractical. Likewise, the most contoured of Everyman's women, Phoebe, falls ill and is in need of help herself, at a time when he wants to pick up again after he cheated on and lied to her—like every man?—and thus provoked the separation. Or Everyman pushes away his friends and relatives because his envy becomes predominant with increasing age. He focuses on the most loyal caregiver, his brother Howie, whom he does not envy wealth or family, but instead his devastatingly good health. This is the secular form of loneliness in the process of ageing which Hofmannsthal introduced as the existential loneliness in dying. Subtly, the medical care also develops in parallel as a process of being left alone: instead of care—a love affair develops with Maureen, a nurse—anonymous medicine is used, where no human faces are visible behind the surgical masks.

Instead of an end

Through *Everyman*, Philip Roth has held up a mirror for every reader to recognise themselves; perhaps the medieval mirror of the mystery play once had similar effects. In Hofmannsthal's play, the mirror has become blunt in some respects, and the mirror image is replaced by the backward ideal of a gracious solution. The art of the novelist Roth, who does not offer us solutions, but rather presents ageing and dying in a highly individual but also generalisable way, is not to moralise or demonise this mirror image. Like Camus' Sisyphus, we might also regard Everyman, despite all decay, as a happy person. Generalisable? In the end, this question remains open: is Everyman the human being, or is Everyman *every man*? Of course, everyone must die, man or woman, but whether sexualisation is used as a defence against ageing, whether loneliness and the impossibility of giving up self-centredness applies equally to every woman, that remains to be seen.

CHAPTER 7

Body, deficiency, shame—*Nemesis* (P. Roth)

The following chapter begins with a fable; it is the story of the "Three donkeys" or of "The miller, his grandson and the donkey".[1]

Wide plain, dusty road. A grandfather walks beside his donkey on whose back his eight-year-old grandson sits. Two hikers come towards them. They say: "Peace be with you, grandfather. But what happens here? The boy having good, strong legs rides the donkey and lets you walk?" To the boy, they say, "Shame on you." The boy gets off and lets the grandfather ride. After a while, they meet two wanderers again. "Peace be with you, my boy." But to the grandfather they say: "Aren't you ashamed? You sit on the donkey and let the poor child walk beside you?" The grandfather says: "Come, my boy, the wanderers are probably right. Get up, sit behind me." After a while, they meet two more wanderers who

---

[1] https://en.wikipedia.org/wiki/The_miller,_his_son_and_the_donkey; last downloaded 29 December 2021.

are outraged: "A disgrace! Two healthy people on an old donkey! Have you no pity for the suffering creature?" The grandfather and his grandson descend. The wide plain, the dusty road. The rest of the way, they carry their donkey.

The fable points out that one cannot escape shame—three asses! Hardly any other emotion has such diverse consequences for one's own experience and actions, and the judgement or condemnation by others, in the fable represented by the wanderers. In the end, you have to carry the donkey yourself.

Nemesis

Nemesis by Philip Roth is a short novel set in the 1940s, as so often in Philip Roth's books, in Newark, New Jersey, USA. The text portrays the fate of a young man during and after a polio epidemic told from the perspective of an acquaintance. This narrator hardly appears in the text; only in the end does it become apparent that he has suffered a fate very similar to the protagonist but has worked it through quite differently. He nevertheless remains detached from the protagonist and only observes, he does not intervene or help.

My thesis is that the text can be best understood through an analysis of shame and its vicissitudes, and vice versa—the novel itself enriches the psychology of shame. First of all, it seems significant that shame is caused by physical suffering. Secondly, the text deals with a particularly shame-sensitive phase of life: late adolescence. Thirdly, the text allows one to recognise how important the other person is for the emergence and the consequences of shame, and that this holds true for generations; accordingly, in the novel, the transgenerational aspect plays a significant role. The feeling of shame has its own history and its own "fate", that is, it is specifically processed and shapes the development of life history. In analogy to the term "vicissitude" concerning the fate of instincts, I will speak of the vicissitudes of shame to emphasise the biographical dynamics of shame. Finally, compared to other novels dealing with shame, *Nemesis* is much more pessimistic, as it deals with the destructive power of shame if it is not integrated psychologically.

On the psychology and psychodynamics of shame

In the following, three dimensions of shame are emphasised: the connection between body experience and shame, the importance of the other in the experience and processing of the sense of shame, and finally handling the experience of lack or imperfection. These dimensions are central to any analysis of shame; they allow the diversity of shame phenomena to be collated and placed on a common theoretical basis.

Body experience and shame

How fundamental the connection between bodily experience and shame is can best be explained with reference to the Judeo-Christian tradition and the first chapter of Genesis. The myth of paradise originally links the first awareness of physical nakedness and shame.

> Adam and Eve "opened both their eyes, and they realized that they were naked." This is shame. In the shame that which one is ashamed of is to be covered: they make themselves an apron. And shame triggers the desire to hide oneself in toto: Adam and Eve hide themselves from God "under the trees of the garden". In shame one is afraid of being looked at, especially by a higher instance. This means: we cannot become human beings without identifying and embodying ourselves, and we can do so only under the conditions of shame. In this almost three-thousand-years-old narrative, shame is regarded as something so fundamental that the dichotomy emanates from it, according to which everything that appears can be a concealment of what withdraws and hides itself. Nothing but being naked—without apron, without hiding, without linguistic evasion—is terrible. It is the origin of suffering—the expulsion from paradise of shameless nudity and innocent names. It is the curse of life, work and pain, enmity and loss of peace. Let them be cast out into it, not without God first making clothes for the poor and naked, as if to show them that this will be their lot: disguise. God made Adam and his wife skirts of hides and clothed them with them (Gen 3:21).
>
> (Böhme, 1997, p. 220)

The fact that experiencing one's own (naked, damaged, imperfect) body can trigger feelings of shame is the reason why two stages of life are particularly prone to shame: childhood and adolescence, on the one hand, and old age, on the other. Both periods of life require an adaptation of identity, as bodily functions and competences either develop anew (adolescence) or are lost (old age). In childhood and adolescence, a stable body image develops and stabilises; new bodily functions and competencies are acquired, learned, and practised. Additionally, sexual development plays a decisive role in this process. Many languages refer to the relationship between shame and body in their vocabulary, and this holds true especially for the relationship between shame and the sexual body. In German, for example, you speak of the pubic area as the "shame region".

In old age, physical and mental functions may become increasingly limited; motor weaknesses, cardiac or respiratory failure, or organic brain processes may lead to uncoordinated behaviour or interfere with the normal use of language. Increased physical, psychological, and social shame can be the resulting consequences, which can intensify social disintegration. The failure may be noticed, but it may also be denied, thereby provoking a "shame spiral": inadequate behaviour is denied—the denial is perceived as a defect by others—the mirror image (deficient, maybe demented) provokes a renewed shame, and so forth.

The importance of the other in the experience of shame

One can only be ashamed of oneself via the gaze of the other, be it real or imaginary. I am ashamed because the other could discover my nakedness and thus expose me. The German language is very precise here: a synonym for *Beschämung* (shaming or embarrassment) is *Blossstellung*, and *bloss* is a synonym for nakedness. If you provoke feelings of shame in another person, they will feel exposed or naked (*bloss*).

Psychoanalytic developmental psychology confirms this phenomenological analysis. Let us begin with the significance of the other for the development of the body image. In the beginning, there is no experience of one's own body, but rather the experience of the "body in connection with others" (Küchenhoff & Agarwalla, 2012), when viewed from the object-relationship perspective, or the "intercorporeality/

intercorporéité", as the French philosopher Maurice Merleau-Ponty (1965, p. 168) stated. Jacques Lacan has shown in his work on the "mirror phase" that the ability to perceive one's own body via one's proprioceptic nervous systems comes late compared to the visual anticipation of a holistic body image as a mirror image. It primarily shapes itself in interaction with others—the other is perceived in its wholeness before the self, and this visual perception is then introjected. As a consequence, the body image as a totality is always preliminary and remains brittle.

Shame appears first in the process of individuation during the phase of intersubjective relatedness in the second half of the first year of life (Stern, 1985). The difference between shame and disgust is interesting from the point of view of developmental psychology. Feelings of disgust indicate that there is something in me that I want to throw out—that which arouses disgust should not belong to me and has nothing to do with me. Or vice versa: what I sacrifice in order to allow separation of object and self becomes the disgusted residue for which Julia Kristeva has created her own term: "abject" (Kristeva, 1980). Disgust has to do with the process of subject–object differentiation. In the case of shame, this has been already achieved. That which I am ashamed of belongs to me in some way, and I cannot simply get rid of it. It is perceived by others, so it belongs to me and yet is accessible to others. Shame, unlike disgust, does not establish the boundaries between me and the other in the first place, they have already been built—but it serves to strengthen and fortify the boundary between subject and object. I feel caught, I know it is myself who is caught—on the other hand, the gaze of the other burns on my soul, but I cannot detach myself from it as long as I am ashamed. Shame and the (imagined) behaviour of the other, preferably the gaze of the other, belong together.

Human development is further influenced and regulated by shame again and again during the entire life cycle. Shame can be understood as a "life-supporting border guard" between the self and the other, subject and object, foreign and familiar. Shame can be seen as a developmental constant—it presents itself as a socially effective and particularly self-reflexive emotion, which presupposes knowledge of one's own person and how one is perceived from an outside position. There is always necessarily a real or imagined observer whose gaze is fantasised as negative or at least critical and judgemental. Shame regulates the self in its relationship to the self and in its relationship to the environment.

In the context of an emotional relationship, shame is also crucial for maintaining a self-concept. In the field of tension between self-awareness and self-expectation, it serves as a protection for the core self's integrity and the perception of identity. It is a signal for the ego to maintain its identity, and it indicates a confusion or an insecurity that manifests itself in vegetative or motor reactions, that is in physical reactions. Shame can be described as bipolar, in which one pole is the subject, the ego and ideal self, in the case that one is ashamed of something, and the other pole is the object, in which one is ashamed in front of another in the relationship (Bohleber, 2008, p. 832).

Shame can thus preserve identity—protect it, in a broader sense. Self-esteem and self-protection can be considered two different aspects of narcissism. Wurmser (1981) also speaks of "protective shame", which protects the core of one's own integrity and is the guardian of human dignity (Wurmser, 1981, p. 6574). From a philosophical and anthropological point of view, Max Scheler (1987) regards shame as a genuinely human feeling, which results from the nature of the human being as a physical and spiritual entity. He understands shame as a "protective effect" and always sees it in relation to the feeling of a positive self-worth.

> Scheler … describes the feeling of shame as (1) an individual's feeling of protecting herself (Schutzgefühl) and her "individual value against the entire sphere of the universal" … The idea that shame is a protective feeling corresponds to the notion that it has a certain potency, capable of rising—to a degree—above the tension … Of course, the impulse to protect entails a sense of something worthy of protection. Shame accordingly also involves (2) a feeling of the value of oneself (Selbstwertgefühl), a feeling akin to (but, nonetheless, distinct from) the related feeling of honor (Ehrgefühl). Shame, on this account, includes an individual's feeling of her own unique value combined with the feeling of safeguarding—and being able to safeguard—herself and this value against the threat of being solely defined by the very same universal (generic, public) characteristics that admittedly co-define who she is.
>
> (Dahlstrom, 2017, p. 252)

Shame and the experience of lack

Often various forms of shame are differentiated in the psychological literature, such as existential shame, competency shame, intimacy shame, shame as the result of a humiliating experience, and idealistic shame as the expression of the discrepancy between the ego and the ego-ideal (Higgins, 1987). This diversity can be confusing, but it summons us to not lose sight of what is unifying, and this can be found in the content of shame. Shame is always connected with something lacking: the right to live, competence, protection, demarcation, the possibility of fulfilling the demands placed on the person who is ashamed. Every subjectively experienced deficit can trigger feelings of shame. Only when we become aware of this connection between lack and shame will it be evident why it makes sense to speak of existential shame. It can be traced back to the ubiquitous fragility of the self, to the psychological vulnerability, and to the incompleteness of satisfaction or other dissonances in human life, that is, to the lack that is inherent in being human.

The psychoanalytic conception of lack does not completely coincide with the anthropological one just outlined. The "lack of being" (Lacan, 1949) in psychoanalytic terms is not provided by the "*conditio humana*" in general, but by the unconsciousness of a large part of our experience. What is unconscious, by definition, cannot be immediately transferred into consciousness, or perhaps not at all. Everything that cannot be easily or completely integrated by the subject in intentions and consciousness can be the starting point for the experience of shame. As the vital ground of the subject, sexuality and desire are only partially conscious, and hence may be outside the subject's control and availability. It may make itself felt where it should not—thus, sexuality may stimulate shame.

If the sense of shame is related to the subjective certainty of having a deficit, a blemish, however human it may be, a failure, and so on, then the defence of shame must ensure that this blemish—this lack—is not experienced and cannot be perceived by the other, and thus, the lack is denied. One form is ruthlessness towards oneself, which may have to do with covering up a deficit. But masochism can also be used to defend against shame; then, the lack is idealised, one enjoys the suffering caused by lack, and in the exaggerated devotion to suffering, the (hidden) exhibitionism appears again—an exhibitionism of lack, as it were—as grandiosity in suffering.

It is not by chance that we have connected not only sexual experience but body experience generally with shame as well. The body as a whole is unavailable to consciousness. This is true in several respects, of which I will provide a short reminder. One's own body cannot become the object of one's gaze as a whole. Physical processes elude arbitrary control to a very large extent, and another person may perceive something physical about me before I do. An excellent example of this is blushing, which I cannot control and which signals my shame, but which in itself also causes shame.

The following principle applies to the analysis of feelings of shame: the less it is possible to integrate the deficiency—in whatever form—the more pronounced the resulting shame and the greater its negative effect will be.

For the analysis of *Nemesis*, as well as for psychotherapy in general, it is also important to consider who can help in what way to relativise the claims to perfection and flawlessness that cause shame and to reconcile with the experience of lack.

Unprocessed shame in *Nemesis*

A short summary reminds the reader of the novel *Nemesis*.

The protagonist of the novel is called Bucky Cantor, but his story is told by Arnie Melzikoff, a former student of Bucky's. In 1944, Bucky became supervisor of the sports field in the Jewish district of Newark, New Jersey. All his friends went to war, but because of a serious eye defect, he was declared "unfit". Bucky therefore provides his sports service all the more thoroughly and devotedly. Soon, the first cases of polio appear. A short time later, two of Bucky's boys fall ill with polio and die within a few days, as the number of cases continues to rise. Bucky is engaged to Marcia, who persuades him to come to a summer camp with her and take over the vacant position of a swimming instructor. He leaves his job and the boys entrusted to him to go with her. Finally, while at the summer camp, he too becomes a carrier of the deadly disease, which he had been spared until then. In the end, Bucky falls ill. Disabled and lonely, he separates from Marcia so as not to hinder her. In Greek mythology, "Nemesis" is the fate that has been assigned to a person. Nemesis is the goddess of justice; Hesiod connects her closely with Aidós—shame. Nemesis punishes hubris, and above all else, human hubris. Thus, Nemesis also appears as the goddess of revenge. Roth's *Nemesis* is a novel in which shame is resonant from the outset.

The world of Greek tragedy is also present in the novel's literary structure. *Nemesis* is an analytical novel, in the sense that the question of guilt is posed and answered by the guilty person himself, as it is in the Sophoclean Oedipus drama or in Heinrich von Kleist's *The Broken Jug*. No one—or hardly anyone—else blames Bucky, only he turns against himself. He uncovers his own guilt or accuses himself of guilt.

However, the question of guilt is left open. Unlike in the Oedipus drama, unlike in *The Broken Jug*, no answer is given as to who might be responsible. Whether Bucky Cantor is in fact the one who spreads polio in the two places where he is staying, whether he—and not the mentally ill person in his district (who only calms down when he is given a hand)—has infected the children he should have protected, whether he carried the virus with him when fleeing to the summer camp where he finds his fiancée Marcia—all this remains open. Mr Cantor, as the narrator—the student also struck by polio—usually calls him, is firmly convinced that he will eventually take the alleged blame.

In the beginning, of course, there is shame rather than guilt. It is difficult to name a shameful primary event since shame goes far back into the family history. Bucky lost his mother at birth, and his father is a delinquent drunkard. The child was therefore shamed by his parents from the outset. The grandfather, with whom Bucky grew up, inoculated him against his parental situation through high ideals of independence and strength:

> The grandfather saw to the boy's masculine development, always on the alert to eradicate any weakness that might have been bequeathed—along with the poor eyesight—by his natural father and to teach the boy that a man's every endeavor was imbued with responsibility.
>
> (2010, p. 223)

The fact that he killed a rat with a shovel as a child is celebrated as the heroic deed that will make him a man and earn his name, Bucky. Bucky, by the way, is the nickname of a comic series, *Captain America*, that was started in 1940, which deals with heroic deeds of the US Army during the war. In addition to this, Bucky's extreme short-sightedness is another cause for him to feel ashamed—the physical flaw that prevents him from becoming a war hero. He is unfit for military service and is terribly ashamed of it. To compensate, he puts all his honour into his well-trained athletic body, the perfection of his swimming skills, and the educational care of the children, to whom he devoted himself during the polio epidemic in the 1944 sports camp, both in sporting and human terms. "His was the body" (p. 279) is stated at the very end of the novel.

Behind the personal lack and parents' deficits, however, the Jewish destiny Philip Roth reflects in all his books is still present as the third layer of causes for shame. Cantor is Jewish, and during the polio epidemic, racist prejudices are awakened when it comes to finding the culprits of the disease. The shame (besides the pride) of being a Jew in a foreign culture—the desire to hide one's Judaism runs like a thread through Philip Roth's books. Already in *Portnoy's Complaint* (1994), the reader might encounter sentences like this one: "I can lie, lie about my name and school, but how am I going to lie away this shitty nose?" (p. 103), and of course this refers to the stereotype of the big Jewish nose (see Tenenbaum, 2006). For many reasons, feelings of shame dominate Bucky Cantor, and he fights against them with all his strength, especially by mastering his own body and by adopting a heroic attitude as an educator.

As the epidemic continues to spread, Bucky follows Marcia's urging pleas and quits his job, leaving his area of responsibility—his replacement for his longing to go to war—to become a swimming instructor at the summer camp, Indian Hill, where Marcia and her two sisters are staying. There he experiences the happiness he has always wished for. He had already got engaged in Newark, he admires Marcia's father, a doctor, who appreciates him, who always and everywhere radiates peace, and who quickly becomes the father he always longed for. But shame also gets hold of him in the summer camp. He tries to chase it away, to deny the feeling of having failed once again—until finally the infection arrives in the summer camp as well, which until then had been idyllic, beautiful, clean, and committed to Native American values. Bucky is diagnosed positive, after asking for a test, and soon he becomes symptomatic.

Now his body is paralysed, dependent, and ugly. Bucky withdraws completely, but above all, he now rejects Marcia, who wants to stand by him, as does her family. Bucky, it seems, takes over his destiny, but in a completely different way than the narrator Arnie, who gets married despite his polio-related disabilities and remains socially integrated. Unlike in the Oedipus drama, however, condemnation is self-imposed, rather than having stemmed from an outside source—Bucky inflicts it on himself.

As in a psychoanalytic cure, further understanding is guided by the details, the seemingly small incidents, which might be quickly over-looked, but which are nevertheless initially puzzling. First, we learn little about Bucky's mother; a small scenic story told by the grand-mother leaves the strongest impression: as a five-year-old, the mother sat down in a basin of water that was by no means as clean as a swim-ming pool is supposed to be. The basin was briefly storing fresh fish before they were to be killed and processed. The novel does not evolve according to psychological or analytical concepts, but this scene nev-ertheless remains psychologically significant. The mother could not allow herself to separate the pure and the impure; instead, she wanted to link the death-prone and the live elements. She is the inhabitant of an intermediate space, but Cantor will spend his whole life searching for purity. The scene that defines his character best is the encounter with an animal: the action by which he earns his grandfather's recognition con-sists of slashing a rat with a shovel. The resulting bloodbath, the splash-ing organs of the rat, are quickly washed off and removed—there is no intermediate area, rather, only a constant fight against the dangerous, the dark, the magic. Thus, Bucky fights against an epidemic, the causes of which are still largely unexplored. He had earned high recognition when he was a sports coach, as he cleaned the sidewalk and chased away the young people who had come into the neighbourhood and spat on the sidewalk with the intention of spreading pathogens. But neither in thought nor in reality does he succeed in separating the dirty and the clean, the good and the bad, that is, he cannot maintain his splitting defences. This is the reason that his failure could enter the radiantly beautiful summer camp: if he is no longer sterile himself, if he is dis-abled and infected, then he is no longer worth anything, and the stigma that he has always fought against has caught up with him. (The novel is a linguistic masterpiece as well, because purity and dirt, health and illness, are polarised again and again using the appropriate words, and every now and then, they merge.)

Throughout the novel, shame is more important than guilt. With good reason, the question of guilt remains unanswered. The assumption of guilt appears as a grand gesture, just like self-condemnation. The narrator is right when he reproaches Bucky's grandiosity in self-dramatisation, "stupid hubris" (p. 208). But this means that the assumption of guilt is not an acknowledgement of guilt, but rather a grandiose gesture with which, in turn, shame is repelled. Arnie reflects towards the end of the novel: "The guilt in someone like Bucky may seem absurd, but in fact is unavoidable. Such a person is condemned. Nothing he does matches the ideal in him. He never knows where his responsibility ends" (p. 273). Bucky almost completely avoids the others' gaze in his further life—he does not expose himself to them anymore. By confessing his guilt, he becomes Marcia's saviour in his own imagination: he does not want her to be crippled, so he separates himself from her and sets her free. Here, once again, a great gesture emerges; though it admittedly turns completely negative, it does affirm the heroism his grandfather was committed to, but at the same time neglects the maternal in-between. All that remains is the dirt and the memory with which the novel ends: Cantor's great athletic qualities when he was still healthy, his skill in throwing the javelin that brings him near Heracles. Deficiency is not integrated into his identity; rather, he uses it for a new self-definition via his grandiose gesture of self-blame. Now Cantor fights against the pure, on the side of the impure. But shame needs mediation, which is exactly what is missing—the narrator turns out to be someone who knows Cantor well in every respect, but who cannot help him to integrate the lack.

Conclusion

In the novel, shame is caused by physical stigma, by myopia, in a particularly shame-sensitive phase of life: late adolescence. The experience of shame and how to deal with it—we have spoken of "vicissitudes of shame"—is embedded in a transgenerational and an intersubjective context. The significance the other person has for the processing of shame seems to be particularly impressive and important for a psycho-dynamic view of shame.

Where others are damaged or feel damaged, like Bucky's relatives in *Nemesis*, or where they appear uninvolved and all-knowing, like the narrator Melzikoff, it becomes difficult to deal with the lack. The fascination of Philip Roth's novels stems from the fact that they relentlessly depict the drama of loss and lack. *The Human Stain* (2001) already pinpoints the deficiency that comes with dark skin in its title. *The Humbling* (2009) tells of the actor who can no longer fill his roles. Lastly, in a literary tradition leading back to medieval allegorical plays, *Everyman* (2005) portrays the life and death of a person dying of a vascular disease. Roth does not write about reconciliation, but he knows the counterforces, especially sexuality, as an antidote in the struggle against the anxiety to dissolve, and against loss in general. He abstains from any illusion and does not insinuate any final solution; on the other hand, he sympathises with all efforts to cope with "human stains". The daughter of the protagonist in *Everyman* cites at his funeral the father's maxim, which sums up this message well: "There's no remaking reality … Just take it as it comes. Hold your ground and take it as it comes" (Roth, 2005, p. 12).

CHAPTER 8

Relations, work on relationship, missed encounter—*The Vegetarian* (Han K.)

E ncounter and relationship—how can one differentiate these terms? There are no clear definitions to distinguish them, and all too often they are used synonymously. And yet a comparison of the two terms suggests a difference in nuance.

First, the term *relationship*. It is not a *terminus technicus* in psychiatry and psychotherapy. Relationship is not even restricted to contact between people. On the contrary, relationships are basic characteristics of life processes. Every life process takes place in an environment; life is bound to exchanges with the environment surrounding the life process. A fairly general definition of relationship characterises it as an exchange between a natural object and its environment or environments; however, these exchanges can differ enormously in their spatial and temporal dimensions. The geological transformation of a mountain is not clearly observable because it extends over an enormous period of time. The relationship between a drying tulip and its environment is quite different: if we fill its empty vase with water, we can observe the consequences of the plant–environment interaction almost immediately, namely when the flower stem tightens and the flower straightens up.

Living beings are attuned to their environments; they react to them and shape them in turn. When living beings are viewed in isolation from the environment with which they interact, they are more difficult to understand; the decision as to what is considered an environment and what is considered indispensable is—and this may be surprising—arbitrary. Every visit to a zoo makes this finding vividly clear: no matter how large the enclosure for a herd of elephants, it is hardly considered species-appropriate today, whereas forty years ago, nobody really regarded it as animal cruelty—not even in the case of circus elephants. In both cases, the elephants have a tiny fraction of the freedom of movement compared to those in the wild. The subjective assessment of what is species-appropriate is an involuntary act that is dependent on emotions and usually not based on scientific findings.

How important the relationship with the environment is for humans has become evident to all of us again since we were forced to realise that the human-environment relationship is endangered by global warming. The self-inflicted destruction of natural living conditions bears witness to the potentially catastrophic consequences of neglecting or ignoring environmental relations. Relationships are interdependent; if the natural environment is to survive man-made interventions, the consequences of controlling nature and its repercussions on mankind must be taken into account.

The quality of interactions changes fundamentally when considering relationships between human beings. If relationships are generally understood as interactions, it is not always easy to distinguish between actor and re-actor, between the acting person and the person acted-upon, that is, subject and object. Weighing up polarity in relationships and deciding its distribution is not naturally granted or pre-configured, rather, it is a central part of relationship dynamics. The communication experts Watzlawick, Beavin, and Jackson (1967) have spoken of punctuation: the circularity of mutual action is subdivided arbitrarily. "The nature of a relationship is dependent on the punctuation of the partners' communication procedures" (p. 69f). How communication is thus shaped, enabled, or prevented shapes the quality of the interpersonal relationship.

Now to the term *encounter*. Encounter seems to be the term that is, on one hand, narrower and, on the other hand, broader, but apparently also deeper than the concept of relationship. It is narrower because it refers more directly to interpersonal communication. It is broader, because encounters don't necessarily need assumptions and definitions, and they encompass a wider circle of possible interactions. An in-depth analysis reveals that encounters can be understood as interactions that are more unbiased, more holistic, and less characterised by instrumental rationality than other forms of relationships.

The German psychopathologist and philosopher Karl Jaspers has drawn a dividing line between therapeutic and existential communication. The latter arises from the purpose-free encounter of people who open themselves to each other, or rather, who find each other in their life reality, while the therapeutic relationship—according to Jaspers (1932, 1989)—is purpose-oriented and can therefore never be an encounter in the precise sense.

Encounters are lived more explicitly in the present and are linked to fulfilling moments, but are linked above all with the shared interpersonal situation, just as the philosopher of religion Martin Buber (1970) distinguished the I–you relationship from the I–it relationship. The I–you relationship constitutes a shared reality, so that I and you are formed first of all from the in-between space of encounter. "All actual life is encounter", emphasises Buber (1970, p. 18). This is a fundamental proposition that needs to be elucidated first. We develop vitality only when we really encounter each other. We always create ourselves anew in encounters with others—if we allow for a deep encounter. Michael Theunissen, one of the great philosophers of the second half of the twentieth century, outlines the Buberian position briefly and succinctly as "the birth of partners from the event of encounter" (Theunissen, 1965, p. 273). Interpersonal encounters do not take place between individuals who define themselves as persons independently of the relationship. Encounters in turn shape the personality of the relationship partners. Self-definition not only precedes the encounter but follows it just as much.

In the following, I will show that encounter and relationship in therapy must be considered conjointly; the therapeutic relationship refers to the specific therapeutic work, and encounter to an existential intersubjective communication. Therapy is characterised by an oscillation between encounter and relationship, which can be understood in the sense outlined above. When offering therapy, therapists get involved with the people who come to us, we meet them as therapists, we allow the therapeutic sessions to be formed by their communication, and we allow ourselves and our patients to develop together. And yet, the relationship between us remains asymmetrical; we use the encounter to draw conclusions that are explicitly more focused on the patient than on ourselves, we remain in a certain neutrality, we share much less of the personal history than the patient does. On the other hand, we cannot work therapeutically with the relationship if we have not encountered each other. The German word *Begegnung* means to have someone opposite oneself, to approach someone approaching me. Encounter is also always about being involved with the other person, about reacting to someone or being impressed by the other, possibly without immediately knowing and noticing this. The therapeutic relationship is not only shaped by the therapist, but also by the therapist's actions in response to the patient's contributions, and vice versa. This encounter is necessary for the therapeutic relationship to have the emotional power through which it can finally bring about changes and a new beginning.

Summing up, it is appropriate to state that in the therapeutic situation, we engage in encounters in order to take them as the basis for the relationship work. Even linguistically, it would sound bumpy if we said that we were getting involved in encounter work—this seems to be a contradiction in terms.

Missed encounters and deadly relationships

Instead of presenting a case study from everyday clinical practice, I will briefly introduce and discuss a contemporary novel, which has rightly received the Man Booker Prize and is important for our topic. It is called *The Vegetarian* and is written by Han Kang (2015), a South Korean author. It depicts the life of a woman who at first stops eating meat, then rejects any contact with animal products, and, finally, after trying to transform herself into a plant, she ends up in a psychiatric clinic where she has to be force-fed. Anyone who treats severely anorexic patients will be reminded of patients with eating disorders, and this will seem strangely familiar. And yet even experienced therapists will be surprised.

The book is artfully constructed and characterised by the fact that no one is blamed, no one is accused or excused, and no diagnostic labels obstruct the view or moderate the brutality of the event. In an extremely factual and therefore highly irritating style, a world unfolds that reminds many reviewers of Kafka, who, in *The Metamorphosis*, meticulously recorded the transformation of a human being into a beetle. In Han Kang's work, a person, driven by dreams, wants to become a plant, and the book is a factual, and therefore merciless, report of this process.

The novel is divided into three parts, each of which portrays the protagonist from the perspective of an important attachment figure. First is her husband, who has never loved his wife, but who considers her useful and who has nothing more to do with her once she refuses to fulfil his demands in more than one respect. Then comes the brother-in-law, an artist who finds his sister-in-law very erotically attractive and makes her the object of a joint work of performance art: he paints her body with plant motifs and lets her have sex with another man, whom he has also painted, in order to finally—because it does not work well—make love to her himself. All these scenes are captured on video, and the films form the work of art. In the third part, the sister, who has separated from her husband, visits the patient, who is about to die in the hospital; she only visits rarely, out of a sense of obligation, and uses the time for self-investigation, by questioning her own life situation.

The biographical background is also provided in the text: in her childhood, her father killed her disobedient dog and forced her to eat the animal's flesh. He forces her to eat meat again when she is already married, after learning of her decision not to eat or prepare any more meat—brief indications of brutality in the family relationships. What is decisive, however, are not the experiences in her former biography. Rather, the missed encounters are important—the relationships that become more and more subtle but always miss the vegetarian's personality. One might hope that, as an artist, the brother-in-law would try to emancipate himself together with the protagonist, and some critics have also understood his actions as participation in a rebellion against the principle of the father or convention. It seems different to me: the artist reduces his sister-in-law to an object in his own way. She becomes an object of his desire, both sexually and artistically. And even her sister, reflective and well-meaning as she may be, does not address the ill sister as a person, because her thoughts revolve around her own life above all else. She cannot find a way out of the role she has been playing in the family, which is to help everyone: once again, she wants to help, and yet she must realise that the vegetarian's personality is based only on the negative, in the rejection of all carnal life.

The novel is about missed encounters, and they are staged in a fascinating artistic and aesthetic way. The protagonist is certainly a Korean woman, so that one could be misled to assume that the novel describes culture-bound attitudes. Instead, she can be read across all cultures as the other person, *par excellence*. This other person remains alone in a deeper sense, as no relationship partners see her as an independent person in her own right. Instead, others reduce her to an object of their desires and expectations.

The psychiatric institution that ultimately takes in the protagonist cannot do justice to her radical search for autonomy, which can be found only in her radical negation—in denying all efforts to help. Nevertheless, the task that we as therapists have to face, even in less extreme cases and on a daily basis, is to start out from the failed encounters, from the "habitual, dysfunctional relationship patterns" (OPD, 2009) and to try to work on them. In doing so, it is important—and this is why I have dealt intensively with concepts of negativity in recent years— that we are also able to see the productive power in seemingly negative symptoms that are produced in the face of unbearable circumstances, for example, the intention for self-preservation. In the apparently deficient, apparently destructive or self-destructive actions, a quest for self-rescue might be detectible (see Küchenhoff, 2013).

A final note about the book: the author has rightly avoided making the protagonist a heroine who is fighting secretly for human autonomy and freedom. This is mirrored in the structure of the novel. The vegetarian does not actually make a personal appearance, rather, she is the object of others' internal monologues. Everything revolves around her, but she is not a subject speaking for herself. She only has a voice of her own in the reported dreams, which are unexpectedly interspersed in the text.

A caveat should be kept in mind that the interpretation just given neglects any culture-bound differences between Korean and so-called "Western" cultures. They may become more prominent for other readers; from my point of view, the novel addresses existential problems involved in missed encounters, in the narcissistic reduction of others to self-objects, and so forth. These conflicts may be acted out in culture-bound ways, but they seem to be humane.

The concept of relationship work

At this point, the concept of relationship work will be explained. Relationship work is necessary in order to identify and change missed encounters. The concept relates to substantial theoretical statements, but also has concrete and practical consequences.

Relationship work means not only material, but also personal, investment. Attention and energy are invested in relationship-oriented therapeutic action. Whoever turns to other persons professionally in such a way that they are expected to truly meet them is personally challenged. They will necessarily have to let themselves be questioned by the experiences with others in the course of their professional practice, just as they have the opportunity to grow in their own personality through encounters with others. In psychoanalytic theory, the concept of work is used in a specific way. Originally, it meant the field work of the farmhand, as the Grimms' dictionary explains, then it expanded to include paid labour, and finally mental labour. In psychoanalysis, work is commonly used as a synonym for psychological investment, for example, when talking about the "work of mourning" and "dream work". "Relationship work", in this sense, means personal commitment and shows that therapy is not possible without effort, or passion.

In psychoanalysis and psychotherapy, therapists do not simply devote themselves to relationships in addition to their core task. If, in our treatment concepts, relationship work forms the medium of psychotherapeutic efforts, then dealing with relationships is part of the core business of those who work in therapy. Relationship management is therefore not simply the expression, for example, of polite interaction with patients or a means of enabling a different and central task, but the pivotal task itself. Incidentally, there is a risk in the increasing professionalisation of therapeutic nursing professions: the standards of value are shifting from relationship work to the handling of defined therapeutic techniques.

Relationship work—relationship-oriented therapeutic action—needs working time. To speak of work therefore implies to be allowed to take time. To engage in a conversation with patients in the lounge of the closed ward in an acute care unit, to create possibilities for establishing a relationship in a deeply distressed situation by one's own unobtrusive presence, is an essential part of work and must not be lost in administrative or technical tasks. In a psychotherapeutic day clinic, taking part in the patients' meals in order to improve the relationship climate of the clinic and, moreover, to accompany anorectically ill people, is not a leisure activity, but therapeutic work.

Work is investment. Taking relationship work seriously means investing in the analysis and design of therapeutic relationships. One of these investments is the possibility of team supervision. It is a fault to simply replace supervision with organisational development, as happens in many places. Relationship work is paid work, and it is an important measure of quality for institutions to what extent they financially invest in the relationship.

How can relationship work be sufficiently described? The therapeutic relationship can become effective as an opportunity for a new, independent relationship, that is, it can enable a new experience that can lead to new trust. In this case, we speak of *working with the relationship*. But the relationship work also has the goal of making precisely those relationship patterns visible, which are inadequate and follow idiosyncratic and unconscious patterns, thus missing the actual encounter with the present relationship partner. These patterns may eventually become visible by reflecting on the therapeutic relationship, and only then might it be possible to interpret the relational impasses and allow the patient to find alternative ways to address others. Relationship work is then *work on the relationship* itself.

This distinction is by no means new; Sigmund Freud distinguished in a similar but not-quite-the-same way between the "mild unobjectionable transference" (Freud, 1912b), which can be used as a basis for the joint therapeutic work, and which itself does not have to be dissolved, and the neurotic transference, which is the object of therapeutic work. Later this discussion was continued in two forms. On the one hand, Alexander and French (1946, p. 22) spoke of the "corrective emotional experience" that the analyst's relationship provides for the analytic subject. On the other hand, Greenson (1965) thoroughly addressed the distinction between the working alliance and transference neurosis. In the following, both perspectives are considered from the perspective of relationship work, and therefore a distinction is made between working *with* the relationship and working *on* the relationship.

Working with the relationship

A recurrent and reliable finding from psychotherapy research is that the quality of the therapeutic relationship has a clear and distinct impact on the outcome of treatment. So, how well therapist and patient get along decides, notwithstanding all specific therapeutic work, whether the therapy is successful. This also applies to treatment in an inpatient team.

The qualities of the therapeutic working relationship can be divided into supporting, learning, and action factors (cf. Lambert, 2004). Supporting factors include identification with the therapist, the reduction of loneliness, and warmth and respect emanating from the therapist. Learning factors are, for example, the advice of the therapist or exploring the personal view together. Action factors include the encouragement to face fears or the recognition of success.

These factors of the therapeutic relationship, which are common to many therapeutic models, are now therapeutically significant in several respects:

– They form the basis for specific therapeutic work.

If a patient has confidence in his doctor, it is much easier for the patient to follow a recommendation to take, say, a medication even if it might produce side effects than to accept a prescription from an unknown or detached person. In the former case, the positive actual therapeutic relationship remains a basis that often does not need to be specifically highlighted and serves as a stable background for the measures to be advised and implemented together.

– Positive relationships provide a new experience that allows for a correction of the established fears and relationship expectations when it is intensive and long-lasting.

In this case, the relationship itself has a direct positive therapeutic effect; it not only creates the basis for different therapeutic steps but is itself a factor in the healing process. This is the so-called "corrective therapeutic experience".

It should be made clear that a positive relationship cannot be taken for granted and be quickly established by a friendly and benevolent attitude. Rather, it often takes relationship work to maintain and protect the therapeutic relationship against the attacks it may face from the patient's unconscious wishes and drives. It is not without reason that both Kernberg's transference-focused psychotherapy and Linehan's dialectical-behavioural therapy agree that such attitudes and behaviour that disturb or endanger the therapeutic relationship take precedence over all other issues. This sounds so obvious, but it is not.

Clinical vignette

In the psychiatric centre I chaired up until 2018 (Baselland Psychiatry), I introduced so-called "risk conferences": employees who had serious and acute therapeutic problems were requested to call a risk conference within forty-eight hours, in which the core team, the senior physician, the head of the nursing department, and the head physician participated; we met in my office. In these sessions, I occasionally perceived that the therapists tried to maintain an intensive therapeutic conversation on biographically and psychodynamically important issues, wishing to continue the therapy at a time when the patient had already terminated the relationship directly or indirectly. If one partner cuts the threads that hold the relationship together, the other partner can no longer work as if the supporting threads still exist. The crucial point is that this overlooks the "attacks on linking" (Bion, 1959) as the currently most important form of relationship.

Working on the relationship

Therapeutic relationships can be effective as more than stabilising therapeutic factors or new, corrective relationship experiences. They can also be used to reveal internalised relationship patterns and expectations. In this case, relationship work makes relationship forms and pathologies visible, with the aim of working on them in order to ultimately enact change. The repetition of relationship types thus shows itself in the therapeutic relationship.

This is the core of the psychoanalytic concept of transference. The strength of psychodynamic interaction is not only to examine cognitive processes in the therapeutic relationship, but also to investigate relationship dynamics that remain unnoticed or unconscious, and to infer persistent, pathological relationship patterns from them. The transference consists of a complex interplay of current, present relationship experiences and past relationship patterns that are emotionally significant and therefore self-repeating. They present themselves in "scenes" (Lorenzer, 2006), which are the practical life experiences, relationship patterns in dealing with others, that have been unconsciously imprinted on the personality, but which nevertheless exert their influence on relationships and shape interactions. The therapist or team allow themselves to become part of the scenes. They must, as it were, step onto the stage provided by the conversation's therapeutic framework. The therapist is not only a reviewer—they are also a player.

The question of how changes in therapy are initiated is of particular importance. In other words, under what circumstances is relationship work successful or effective? In order to find an answer to this question, I will examine the therapeutic relationship in psychoanalytic therapy as an example; as is well known, it is based on two basic rules: free association on the part of the analysand, and free attention on the part of the analyst. The well-known Freud quote that describes both basic rules is as follows:

> Just as the patient must relate everything that his self-observation can detect, and keep back all the logical and affective objections that seek to induce him to make a selection from among them, so the doctor must put himself in a position to make use of everything he is told for the purposes of interpretation and of recognizing the concealed unconscious material without substituting a censorship of his own for the selection that the patient has forgone. To put it in a formula: he must turn his own unconscious like a receptive organ towards the transmitting unconscious of the patient. He must adjust himself to the patient as a telephone receiver is adjusted to the transmitting microphone.
>
> (Freud, 1912e, p. 115)

This concept is momentous: when the participants in a conversation adjust their unconscious to one another, desire is also integrated into the exchange of words and thoughts. Therefore, psychoanalytic insight is passionate; passion is not only its subject, but also a prerequisite for insight. Many important analytical authors have integrated this thought into their key concepts. For W. R. Bion, desire is connected with cognition, and he therefore chooses the signs of the sexes, for man and woman, to stand for the psychoanalytic cognition worked out together. Bion has understood the way the analyst gives an interpretation (Bion, 1962) as the fruit of a conception, and for this he has used the English double meaning of the word, which can mean "concept" but also "conception". In this way, in the words of philosopher H. Arendt (1958; cf. Durst, 2004), generativity, the new natality, is represented in the analytical conversation, a new beginning not hitherto present in the thoughts and concepts of the participants. Thus, the interpretation is regarded as a "child" of the analytic work, which will be sooner or later independent and will lead its own life (see Britton & Steiner, 1994), and will thus produce independent effects. This idea is found everywhere in contemporary psychoanalytic discussion; examples include Ogden's concept of the "analytic third", or R. Schafer's concept of the interpenetration between analyst and analysand (Schafer, 2000). Like Bion, Schafer's term also emphasises the sexual, instinctive component in mutual fertilisation. In other words, the psychoanalytic conversation is then a "fertile conversation", to use a pertinent metaphor which is common in German, at least.

However, the analysis provides change for the analysand only if it is performed passionately. The analyst must not only engage with the mind, but must also be prepared to enter the therapeutic process as a passionate person. If the analyst accomplishes this, the analysis becomes a risk for them as well. It becomes a journey into the unknown, which also produces unplanned and surprising effects, in which much is at stake for the analyst.

The same can be said in another way: by analysing, I am also analysed. Just as a work of art, for example a picture, is not only seen, but at the same time directs its gaze at us, and we are seen and captured by a picture, so we are questioned and interpreted by the analysand who works with us. Ferenzci (1988) spoke, somewhat unhappily, of mutual analysis. As a technique of manifestly mutual analysis, it has failed, but on the other hand, any analysis is implicitly mutual. Thus, through what I understand as an analyst, I also change, at least in principle. What I understand, perhaps for the first time, affects me, expands my horizon of understanding, and leads to a change. I identify with the person I am analysing, and this identification can enrich me.

I will illustrate the importance of affect in therapeutic work through an example from our own practice.

Clinical vignette

Mrs X has been coming to me for some time in psychoanalytic psychotherapy. I will omit all anamnestic data and emphasise only that the treatment has been enormously burdened by a severe obsessive-compulsive disorder. Here, I will discuss one therapy session in which I lose my patience.

After Mrs X's life had calmed down considerably after hard times of extreme instability, and the relationship with her partner had stabilised, she starts to question again all the choices she has made in recent years, and considers whether she might not have made the wrong decisions from the beginning. I cannot see the factual reason for these new and highly distressing doubts and feel extremely tormented. In this hour, I can no longer stand it after my usual attempts at interpretation have failed to stop the compulsively compelling thoughts. With clear affection, I offer that I think she has to do something like all other people, namely, to take the step of giving up many abstract possibilities in favour of the realisation of one of these possibilities. She does not give our work a chance if she presents the failure of her life's path many years ago as an irrefutable reality. A part of her is reluctant to take part in therapy because she would then have to say goodbye to the highs of adolescence and to her parents. That is why she does not talk about how much she has achieved in her life development.

Through this vehement, overly long interpretation, she calms down. She is relaxed in the hours that follow, reporting on individual works during her studies that she enjoys. Why does my "outburst", my confrontation marked by a somewhat uncontrolled countertransference, which results in too long an interpretation, calm her down? I told her nothing other than what I had often said before in my interpretations, then given in a calmer voice. Certainly, I clearly marked a limit—of my patience—combined with a limit that lies in my appeal and the patient to finally change. In this way, I became more transparent as a counterpart—which was a relief in view of the contourless nature of the early caretakers. Of course, I also protect the therapy; I do not want the destructive side of the patient to oppose the therapy, but the decisive factor seems to be that the patient had a chance to get a better feeling of me. The calm attitude that I had previously adopted (which nevertheless had always been committed and never indifferent on my part) had not reached her. I had not, as it were, overcome her emotional barriers. It was quite different after she experienced me defending the shared therapeutic work, even though I uncontrollably and violently threw interpretations at her. In that moment, she felt my commitment, but also heard my "no", and she could then find herself in this "no", reflect herself in my demarcation, and identify herself with this demarcation.

It seems to me that it is not by chance that time and again such small episodes of "acting out", that is, unplanned and surprising moments of interaction on the part of the therapist, become milestones in analytical therapy.

Ethical dimension of relationship work

Making relationship work the focus of everyday work in psychiatry and psychotherapy is not only a practical measure, but also an ethical decision. If relationships are thought of in such a way that the relationship partners depend on each other, that they mirror each other, influence each other, and even shape their individuality and identity through the relationship, then the concrete implementation of this relationship concept in psychiatry and psychotherapy excludes certain attitudes from the outset, while others necessarily follow from them.

There is no objective, uninvolved, external position in clinical work, or a position independent of relations.

Each observation is not only dependent on the location of the observer but is also relational. What I perceive in the other person also has to do with the attitude I choose towards him.

The other can become the object of my (diagnostic or therapeutic) gaze, but I must be aware that, in this way, I reduce the encounter between two people to a subject–object relationship.

Relationship work follows the spontaneous encounter, but, through reflection, engenders a more distanced contact. Self-reflection of the relationship partners includes the ability and willingness to look at and question—on a so-called meta-level—what has spontaneously established itself between the relating partners.

Relationship work is therefore associated with a necessary critical attitude towards manipulation and violence. It acknowledges that they often cannot be avoided, but demands that every form of heteronomy be accounted for and returned to an equal contact.

Relationship work takes both difference and strangeness into account. It lives from the fact that both dimensions are fundamental as relationship dimensions. Making an effort for the other does not mean permanently "occupying" the other. Nevertheless, every form of relationship contains elements of appropriation of the other person in the first place.

Psychoanalysis still uses the concept of cathexis, which stems from drive psychology. The other as object becomes the object of one's own, possibly unconscious, desire, that is, it is occupied. The German term is *Besetzung*, which has a certain militaristic connotation (occupation). Yet it is adequate and relevant. One's own desire reduces the other to an object. The other something is seen, desired, feared in a way that corresponds to one's own unconscious images. This was portrayed in the second part of the book *The Vegetarian*, but the other as a stranger does not fully coincide with this object function, just as the protagonist of the novel cannot really be seen in the unilateral and appropriating view of the relatives. The result is disappointment on all sides. The three relatives who tell of the protagonist do not have their wishes satisfied.

The person who undertakes psychoanalysis must experience and work through this lack of fulfilment of an unconscious desire. In object-relationship psychological terms: they must recognise that the object of desire cannot fulfil what it is supposed to fulfil. This is connected with disappointment, that is, a resolution of deception. For the therapeutic relationship and transmission, this means that the analyst, desired as an always good mother, is not the incarnation of this mother. Thus, the desire as well as the disappointment inherent in it must be recognised. The other is always different than the object he is supposed to be in the situation of transference. At the same time, the otherness of the other, the distance of the other, precisely in the proximity of desire, must also be recognised. It is about the indissolubility of a remainder that is the otherness of the other.

Psychotherapy, especially psychoanalytic psychotherapy, does not dissolve the tension between (inner) objects and the other. On the contrary, it helps to realise it. Its goal is that objects become others again and again, that is, subjects to whom we establish a relationship, that can be cathected objectively, but are not totally defined by this cathexis, and with whom an encounter will then perhaps be possible. A paradox arises: in therapy, we experience how important object cathexes are. They imply that the other is converted into an object in all kinds of relationships; we cannot stop addressing the other in this way. But we can realise that and in what way we do it. This self-reflexive step also has consequences: the imperative demand on the object to be this or that for me is not replaced by a wishless renunciation but rather by a wish bent back in itself, reflected, but not dissolved. For my relationship to the other, this does not mean that I now look at him without interest—without egoism—only for his own sake, and so on. Nevertheless, I now recognise our difference, and inherent in the recognition of the other's subjectivity is the acceptance of the fact that I cannot completely "grasp" the other.

But because the other remains foreign, he also becomes the object of my curiosity. Jessica Benjamin speaks of the child's desire to connect with external reality. For her, the paradoxical experience of being together and being different is a decisive developmental principle. She describes the capacity to recognise "the difference between the other as subject and the other as object" (Benjamin, 1995, p. 29) as crucial.

Joy in perceiving the independent existence of the other person seems to me to be an additional result of psychotherapy. This is seen in the awakening of curiosity about the strangeness of the world, about the mystery of the other, who as an other repeatedly withdraws. This is a world that is not to be conquered completely, that nevertheless does not have to be experienced in a hostile or unreachable way, even if it cannot be conquered and remains in its own right. And entering into this therapeutic exchange makes encounter possible.

CHAPTER 9

In transition: say goodbye and start over—*The Nix* (N. Hill)

The theme of the following chapter is the transition from a farewell in the broadest sense, which includes separation, loss, and other similar experiences, to a new beginning that reopens the future. The three dimensions—farewell, transition, new beginning—are thereby considered through a temporal perspective. In the first part, which deals with farewells, only one aspect of the many determinants of farewells is highlighted: the great difficulty of psychologically performing a farewell, and this also means ending a farewell in time, when there is no present moment of farewell, no act of saying goodbye, no ritual of saying goodbye. To put it bluntly, we could say that where a farewell is not possible in the present as saying goodbye, the lost other remains present and does not retreat into the past. The reasons as to why this is the case will be given. In the second part, the temporal characteristics of the transition between farewell and new beginning will come into focus—first, how long a transition can or must be so that it can lead to a new beginning after a farewell; and second, whether the temporal relationship between farewell, transition, and new beginning is to be understood as a consecutive sequence of events, or as repetitive and dynamically oscillating so that the sequence is passed through several times repeatedly until it comes to an end. In a third part, the time structure of the new beginning is highlighted by offering clinical-psychoanalytic vignettes, a literary text, and social situations as material.

Impossible farewell and continued presence

If it is impossible to say goodbye, then the person or place being left remains permanently present, so that it becomes difficult to let go and open the experiences of the present to expectations for the future. For this reason, throughout all times and cultures, people have developed rituals of saying goodbye to the deceased. The cultural historian Thomas Laqueur (2015) proved in his large-scale study *The Work of the Dead* that the Greek philosopher Diogenes failed in his conviction that after death every dead body could be thrown over the city walls to be eaten by the wild animals outside, under the assumption that the corpse has no meaning whatsoever, neither for the dead nor for the survivors. Historical and transcultural analysis, on the other hand, shows that the mortal remains of a human being were always cared for and became bearers of meaning, whether in cemeteries, in lists, monuments, or texts. Laqueur emphasises that the work of the deceased is done as a work on time, creating a link between the past and the future. Even urn burials, which are becoming increasingly common, do not contradict these findings. For even when the dead body is burned, it remains present, most often as an image of the deceased next to the urn during the burial or later at the grave (Berger-Zell, 2013).

But what makes it impossible to say goodbye to a loved one who is lost or disappears? I will use examples to name some of the predisposing factors.

Refused farewell

When people say goodbye to each other, it is a reciprocal act, not a one-sided one. When relationships fall apart, there must be a minimum of mutual agreement for the separation to take place. If it is not accepted by both parties, the wish on one side that a future apart from each other should not happen can become the determining factor for action—it may lead to stalking. It is now well known that stalkers cannot end a relationship or marriage, unlike their partners who want to leave.

The victims of stalking, however, may have their share of responsibility for not completing the separation, for example, if they do not state the reasons for the separation, or if they say goodbye abruptly.

More subtle and difficult to grasp, but also fatal in its psychological effects, is the refusal of important caregivers to even acknowledge a separation. I give a clinical example from my therapeutic practice.

Mrs A comes into therapy because she can no longer sleep well. The worries of her demanding professional life will not let her be, and she diagnoses herself with burnout. Soon it becomes clear that the work is so strenuous primarily because Mrs A claims to regulate and control all processes in the company she is in care of by herself. She does not place any trust in the employees, so no one can effectively replace her so that she could be relieved.

Biographically, early traumatisation is crucial. A younger brother is born severely disabled and dies after a few years. The parents devote themselves to him during his short life span without reserves, and there is no attention left for the daughter. After the son's death, the mother becomes more and more entangled in a delusional universe, which the father shares with her, or at least accepts. The daughter, who had initially suffered from being forgotten, is now cathected again, but only as a self-object, which is supposed to share the parents' distorted perception of reality and to work together with them on the combative transformation of reality. Mrs A can build a life of her own only by completely breaking away from her parents in early adulthood and creating a career thanks to an unusually alert intelligence.

Mrs A, we can say, could not build up a sustainable inner object, but rather had to deal with a paranoid inner object instead, from which she always tries to distance herself anew, and which she tries to control or keep in check. This has an effect on her relationships in a seemingly paradoxical way: wherever she starts to invest trust, a relationship becomes unbearably dangerous, and she has to distance herself. This also makes therapy more difficult, although I recognise the deep longing for a supporting object in my countertransference from the beginning. The work of saying goodbye to the pursuing inner object is disturbed and made more difficult by the fact that the pursuing object, which was formed during the early years, is by no means only inside. Even if Mrs A completely renounced her parents decades ago in order to—as she herself puts it—survive, this separation has never been accepted or acknowledged by the parents during her whole lifetime. They leave messages in all ways technically possible, either overwhelming the daughter with reproaches or—even more difficult to bear—sending her orders and requests every day, as if nothing had happened over the years and decades, as if there had never been a break in the relationship. The image of the undead, of the "revenants" or ghosts, imposes itself. The psychological consequences for Mrs A are devastating. Without being psychotic herself, she fears an omnipresent assault or attack by her parents. She cannot enter a permanent and trustful friendship, and remains unmarried. Without being able to defend herself against it, she becomes involved in the parents' delusion. The inner and outer reality intermingle and can hardly be separated from each other.

The impossible farewell to the never-existing object

Saying goodbye is not possible even if the object to be left has never been present. At first, this formulation sounds paradoxical; for under what circumstances can an object that is never present become significant in one's own experience? Nevertheless, there are circumstances that lead to this constellation. The word "object" is helpful for understanding, like the German word *Gegenstand* (object). It describes a counterpart that in some way confronts the subject or has been designed by the subject as an other. But if it is present without being able to be objectified, it cannot be dealt with either; it becomes intangible, incomprehensible, unbelievable.

I will give a clinical example again:

Mrs B does not find out who her father is until she is in her late sixties. Her mother had given her away to a foster family after she was born. Mrs B gets to know her birth mother later in life, and asks about her father, but the mother does not answer the question. The foster parents explain that they know nothing about the father. She develops an amazing power to assert herself in her adult life, she has a job, gets married, and has children —and yet something remains mute and empty in her, however fulfilled life may seem, not least to herself. After her biological mother, who had developed dementia in her last years, dies, Mrs B decides to order and read her child protective service files and to search for her father. It is not easy for her, but finally she reconstructs an image of the father, of whom the foster parents had in fact known, as had her mother, because the files show that the father paid them child support until his daughter came of age. She reads letters that her birth parents had sent each other: they loved each other but could not be together because the father was married. After reviewing the files, she becomes overwhelmed by a great sadness in therapy, and we find out together that she has not simply become depressed, but that the lifelong muteness, the presence of a mute object, has become eloquent and allows for mourning, because the object has now been given a face.

The abrupt loss without the farewell

We have already pointed out how important it is for the mourning process to say farewell to the dead body. That is why an enormous effort is made to search for the dead bodies after catastrophes, even if it is very difficult or even impossible to find them. Processing of railway suicides, which I unfortunately had to deal with again and again in the psychiatric centre I ran until 2018, is also made more challenging by the fact that the bodies are destroyed beyond recognition. Therefore, relatives are often advised not to view the deceased, or what is left of them. But this makes the final goodbye even more difficult.

As an example of an abrupt farewell and its consequences, I chose a contemporary novel to which I would like to draw attention.

The Nix by Nathan Hill (2016) deals centrally with the very topic with which this chapter is concerned: the unfulfilled farewell implies that a replacement cannot occur, and that history repeats itself in the life experiences of the protagonists until the farewell can be accomplished.

The protagonist of the novel is Samuel, a university teacher who is brought down after refusing to give a student a certificate of achievement. He has noticed that she is guilty of plagiarism—as in all her other works, including one of his exams. She, however, provides false testimony that the professor is contemptuous of women. In addition, she searches for material against him, and she finds what she is looking for, because he is in fact addicted to gambling and is networking with a gambling community on the Internet that diverts a great deal of time and attention away from university activities.

Samuel had once had great success through a book publication; a second one has been announced, he lives on the advances, but he doesn't get any work done because he doesn't write, but falls back on gambling instead. Finally, in order to save himself from legal proceedings and money demands from his publisher, he is summoned to tell his mother's story. Many years earlier, she had caused a sensation because she had thrown stones at a right-wing radical presidential candidate. But now Samuel has had no contact with his mother for over twenty years. When he was eleven years old, she disappeared from the family without leaving any message or explanation. He is nevertheless ready to write a new bestseller and to save himself economically, even if he drags his mother's private life into public view. This time, enlightenment is not pursued in the service of humanistic ideals, but out of business necessities. Samuel is an abandoned son, left alone with unsolved questions concerning his very existence. He has been deceived himself, but he cannot escape becoming a cheater, be that in his relationship to his own mother, to whom he feigns personal interest, or the university, his employer, towards whom he feigns research, when he actually prefers an Internet game.

The abrupt end of the relationship with the mother has awakened spirits, the old Nordic spirits—The Nix—of which the mother had told the child. Her departure cannot be mourned because she remains present in her absence, as a spirit, as a void around which the whole of Samuel's life revolves. But he is not aware of the void, and thus cannot limit it. It is replaced by the boundless level of play that reaches out into the universe, wonderfully depicted in the novel, which at the same time provides an analysis of the addiction to play.

Set in three points in time—1968, 1995, and 2011—the novel, which is much more fragmented in its time structure than my retelling would suggest, now reconstructs the life of Samuel's mother after the son sets out in search of her with growing personal interest. And it turns out that she was abandoned in a comparable way: her father, who, now demented, spends his days in a nursing home, had left before the Nazis invaded Norway, in an extremely difficult situation, without saying goodbye to the family. He had the choice between accompanying refugees on a boat and thus saving them and himself, or of abandoning them to their likely deaths and staying with the family, with an uncertain outcome. It was only when the mother understood her father's decision and only when the son followed in the mother's footsteps that everyone's life finally calmed down.

It is not a happy ending that Nathan Hill presents to us: the son has lost his job, the demented father still does not recognise the mother and confuses her with the older daughter left behind in Norway. And yet Samuel develops an ability to enter a tender relationship, indicated by carefully restoring a friendship with a childhood love. This is made possible by the fact that Samuel is able to reconstruct and recount his own life story and that of his mother. The telling of the story allows understanding, and understanding is accompanied by forgiveness:

> So instead of looking for answers, he'd begun simply writing her story thinking that if he could see the world the way she saw it maybe he'd achieve something greater than mere answers: Maybe he'd achieve understanding, empathy, forgiveness.
>
> (p. 66)

He realises that by breaking off the relationship, the mother tore a hole in his psychic fabric that never healed. But by becoming aware of and feeling it, he can begin to say goodbye instead of hating, because hatred also binds and prevents parting. Only now can the protagonist arrive at the present: "He can prevent his past from swallowing the present."

Transition and the time dynamics involved

How should we imagine the transition between a farewell and a new beginning? At first, we can start from a static model, but we will soon proceed to a more differentiated one. The static model can be paraphrased as follows: the farewell has been completed, but the new possibilities in life have not yet been able to develop. The model is useful in one respect because it allows us to consider the time interval that lies between parting and new beginning.

The duration of the transition

A transition must be finite; in order for the prefix "trans" to be used meaningfully, the transition must contain an in-between, an interspace. Better said, in a transitional period, it must be possible—metaphorically speaking—to look from one end (the parting) to the other (the restart). As a corollary, it is possible to determine an optimal and a maximum tolerable transition period. It is easier to illustrate this by means of examples.

We know from infant observation that, varying by age, a child can bear the absence of the object of care for a while because it has the expectation that it will soon return. If this expectation is then not fulfilled, the child will fall into agitation and soon into despair. After a while, it gives up, becomes silent, and has apparently lost sight of the object, as it no longer shows signs of happiness once the object returns. The memory from previous experiences that the object does not let you down helps for a while, since the retained image of the object builds emotional bridges. But it breaks down if the return is delayed too long.

The transitional object, which has become so important in psychoanalytic theory, can help in extending the transition time by serving as a surrogate object for the missed real person. It is no big secret that this does not only apply to children: almost every fifth adult woman (nineteen per cent) and every ninth man (eleven per cent) regularly uses a cuddly toy, as was reported in a survey in 2014 (*Süddeutsche Zeitung*, 16 February 2014).

The significance of the transition period and the possibilities for shaping it remain important, especially in those moments in adult life that are existentially significant. In these moments, there are time intervals that must not be exceeded if a transition is to remain bearable. I will mention two areas as examples:

It is not without reason that German social psychiatry speaks of "transitional homes", which are intended to provide a bridge between the hospital and the unprotected social environment for seriously mentally ill people. Now the question arises whether this term is not a euphemism or simply wrong in many instances (Dörr, 2005). All too often, the two ends of the transitioning bridge are lost when a resident stays in a temporary home for years; the bridge becomes a home, and the transition collapses.

There is also talk of transitional facilities for people who flee their home and apply for asylum. As a rule, they come from intolerable and traumatising situations, have had to break away from home, and do not yet know what life in the host country will be like—whether they can settle in, whether they will be tolerated. How long is this life of uncertainty bearable? In this situation, when does the trust in a protective object disappear? Is the time for processing asylum applications (in Germany in 2017: 10.7 months; DW Akademie, 1 January 2018) tolerable by any means? According to a political agreement from 2018, the duration of an adult's stay in a refugee camp should not exceed eighteen months as a rule (Wikipedia, 23 August 2021). Apparently, this is the period of time that is considered reasonable.

A political study has now also shown that shorter asylum procedures prove to be positive in many respects. The researchers have examined the data of about 17,000 provisionally admitted refugees in the migration information system of the Switzerland State Secretariat for Migration (SEM) between 1994 and 2004. The probability of finding a job decreases by a fifth if the refugee has to wait a year longer for the decision, writes the Swiss National Science Foundation (SNSF) in a statement: "No matter how well educated refugees are, no matter where they come from, old or young—if their lives are put on hold for years, they become discouraged" (Kürzere Asylverfahren reduzieren Arbeitslosigkeit, 4 August 2016).

The dynamics of transition

The previous section discusses a static model of transition, which assumes linear time, in which the farewell is followed by the transition and then by a new beginning. However, this model has its limits, because it does not consider the temporal dynamics of transitions. Farewell and new beginning are intertwined in time. Once again, a look at developmental psychology is helpful in this context. It has already been described that the absence of the object can only be endured for a certain time. In addition to the duration of separation, it is also decisive whether an interplay of independent exploration of the environment and return to the protective reference persons is possible. Margaret Mahler described this reassurance of the child towards the primary object as "checking back" (Mahler, Pine, & Bergman, 1975). It examines whether it is possible, in the process of separation from the primary object, to reassure oneself of the object, not only once, but repeatedly, and this under different conditions through all phases of childhood development. It regresses and progresses continuously and in rapid succession. A dynamic view of transition takes this iterative process into account, in which farewell, separation, and new beginnings are repeatedly tested and played out.

Freud imagined the work of mourning in such a way that, as he says, "Each single one of the memories and expectations in which the libido is bound to the object is brought up and hyper-cathected, and detachment of the libido is accomplished in respect of it" (Freud, 1917e, p. 245). Even if the choice of words suggests that this is a mechanical process in which each connecting knot must be loosened individually, even if mourning is more complex than described in Freud's text about "mourning and melancholia", the formulation still impressively highlights the process's binding and loosening in reference to the steps of mourning that are repeated again and again.

Winnicott spoke of the transitional space and characterised it by its indeterminacy—by its productive intermediate position. It is well known that in the transitional space, the question of where an experience belongs—in the external or internal reality—to the subject or to the object, must be forgotten if it is to open up an intermediate realm of fantasy and artistic productivity. The transitional object is sometimes seen as an external object and sometimes as part of one's own body; however, this does not produce any contradiction or conflict. "Once" and "another time", however, are temporal determinations. Accordingly, the transitional space includes the transitional period, which is characterised not only by a certain duration, but also by loops or spirals of repetition, by a movement to and fro.

The time-dynamic view of transitions has practical consequences, and it can again be illustrated by the demands on doing justice to refugees. Time should be allowed for repetitive spirals in a transitional facility for refugees—spirals that are worthy of the name. Migrants or asylum seekers should be able to claim a transitional period in this dynamic sense, so that they can easily switch between the attachment to their homeland and the object relations of the present host country, so that they can work through the customs of origin and the habits of the host country without being forced to make hasty decisions. They could then learn at an early stage what in culturally sensitive psychotherapy is called "cultural frame switching" (von Lersner & Kizilhan,

2017, p. 22), the ability to switch between the offers and demands of different cultural environments without conflict. Unfortunately, reality is often quite different for the refugees. Quick decisions and choices, for example, where they want to live, are constantly demanded of them. If they want to preserve the home country's culture, holding on to the traditions can obstruct playful exploration of new realities. If they abandon their origins and adapt to the host country, there is potential for the development of a serious identity conflict.

A brief reference to a second novel suggests itself at this point. Lars Gustafsson was an important author in the 1970s, and he published a cycle of five novels, *Cracks in the Wall*, all of which were connected by a motto that describes the dynamics of transition very well and at the same time leads to a new beginning: "We will start afresh. We will not give up." A work of written art as well, each of the novels, especially the last one, titled *The Death of a Beekeeper* (Gustafsson, 1981), captures the back and forth between the familiar and the new, between everyday life and dying, between limiting illnesses and unaccustomed life practices.

The new beginning

In psychoanalytic discussion, the term "new beginning" is closely linked to Michael Balint, who has given the term "new beginning" the status of a technical term, but unfortunately did not elaborate exactly what it confers. Nonetheless, the image of the analysand who did a somersault in Balint's analysis class has become an integral part of the history of psychoanalytic theory. I quote the original passage:

> It took us about two years before these connections made sense to her. At about this time, she was given the interpretation that apparently the most important thing for her was to keep her head safely up, with both feet firmly planted on the ground. In response, she mentioned that ever since her earliest childhood she could never do a somersault; although at various periods she tried desperately to do one. I then said: "What about it now?"—whereupon she got up from the couch and, to her great amazement, did a perfect somersault without any difficulty.

This proved to be a real breakthrough. Many changes followed, in her emotional, social, and professional life, all towards greater freedom and elasticity ...

Accepting that the breakthrough was an important factor in the good therapeutic result, the question arises how to understand its dynamism. The good result might have been brought about by: (a) forcing the consciousness—or the ego—to lift part of the repression and accept an instinctual urge as ego-syntonic and enjoyable; (b) strengthening the ego by extending its boundaries at the expense of the id; and (c) helping the patient to a new beginning or, if preferred, to a stronger ego.

(Balint, 1979, pp. 127, 130)

Balint opens a theoretical parenthesis: he connects the so-called basic disorder (we would speak today of severe personality disorder) with the new beginning. The decisive factor in the situation is his "What about it now?"—his encouraging, but not pressing, intervention to get involved in a new experience, while in his presence. Thus, Balint understands the new beginning as an expression of a new, trusting togetherness, which makes it possible to catch up on experiences of "primary love"—the original bonding, the primal trust—where it was missing, in the case of profound psychological disorders. This close connection between basic disturbance and new beginning was later criticised, and the approach of the new beginning—for example, with Thomä—has been generalised, as a "process in the here and now", as "building up trial treatments on the basis of gained insight in an atmosphere favorable to this" (Thomä, 1984, p. 537). Then the new beginning simply becomes a rehearsal of new behaviour in the present. Even if it seems to make sense to acknowledge phenomena of a new beginning independently of the degree of disturbance in psychotherapy, Balint's basic idea is thus lost. Balint is not concerned with "atmosphere", but with the experience of a loving relationship, which creates and encourages trust and thus makes new experiences possible. This addresses, if not the basic disturbance, then at least the basic trust that is the basis for a new beginning. Secondly, as a process in the here and now, according to Thomä, trial and error becomes practice, while in the somersault and the encouragement leading up to it, in the "What about it now?", a crisis is described that can be used positively or passes away.

Today, the "What about it now?" coined by Michael Balint can also be reformulated as a "now moment". Stern et al. (1998) have described the now moment as a special kind of present moment in which the familiar framework, the well-known interaction with one another, suddenly changes. The interaction spontaneously takes paths that are different from the usual ones, the situation becomes unfamiliar, and it demands a quick, involuntary decision. Stern and his colleagues from the Boston Study Group on the Process of Change describe the development of a now moment as a sequence of three phases:

> Now moments can be described as evolving subjectively in three phases. There is a "pregnancy phase" that is filled with the feeling of imminence. There is the "weird phase" when it is realised that one has entered an unknown and unexpected intersubjective space. And there is the "decision phase" when the now moment is to be seized or not. If it is seized, it will lead to a "moment of meeting", if all goes well, or to a failed now moment if it does not.
>
> (Stern et al., 1998, p. 912)

Now moments are the critical and kairotic moments of experience, containing a *kairós*, in which the therapeutic relationship is questioned, and unexpected new possibilities of encounter are offered, which can be seized or missed. If Balint had, as usual, given an interpretation related to childhood, if the patient had not done the somersault, but had continued to articulate her concerns and inhibitions as usual, the moment of change, that is, of a new beginning, would have passed unused.

The terms that Stern et al. have chosen for the three phases deserve to be taken seriously, as they allow us to define the moments of the present more precisely.

When the impending indefinite is characterised as a pregnancy phase, a future is already introduced—the prospect of something new, of a new beginning, because the arrival of the new is linked with pregnancy and birth in a particularly concise way. In philosophical discussion, it was Hannah Arendt in particular who elaborated natality, birth, as the anthropological basis of the new beginning (Hansen-Löve, Ott, & Schneider, 2014).

The weird phase is not actually characterised by something uncanny, but rather by a fascination for something that lies outside of the usual and is therefore unsettling. In the unfamiliarity of the everyday, there is a distance from, and thus also a potential adoption and negation of, the past. Hannah Arendt speaks of the "abyss of nothingness that opens up before any deed" (Arendt, 1978, p. 207).

Finally, active action belongs to the third and last phase, the phase of decision: this is the stage at which the god Kairós must be seized if he is not to immediately escape again. The fulfilled and changing present moment, which makes a new beginning possible, does not fall to him, but is seized. The "initium" requires initiative in order for it to happen.

Nevertheless, it is essential for a successful present time in therapy, and thus for a new beginning, to be able to rely on the shared history—the long-term development of the intersubjective relationship, which is the prerequisite for creating a transitional space, a space of creativity. The preconditions for the fruitful moment of the somersault were created in the long preceding joint analytical work of Balint and his analysand.

In my opinion, despite the great merits of describing changes in therapy, the basic error of the Boston Study Group is that it places a level of implicit, spontaneous, emotional, and physical relationship *alongside* the analytical work on the transference relationship, and it is precisely this level of relationship that should create moments of encounter and thus change. There are not two relationships in psychotherapy—the shared reflection and the interpersonal, bodily connection do not run side by side, and they cannot be separated from each other. Reflection and interaction are aspects of the one therapeutic relationship, and they interact with each other, so that finally those condensed moments and unplanned encounters are possible, which change, open, and generate something new.

Psychoanalytic psychotherapy exploits the potential of intersubjective bonding, not only to remember, repeat, and work through, but also to prepare a new beginning together. If Hannah Arendt derives the "talent for the absolutely unpredictable" (Arendt, 1958, p. 167) from the fact of being born, which is the new beginning *par excellence,* anchoring the new beginning in the quality of the relationship is not a contradiction. This approach merely goes back one step further, as it were, from birth, backwards to procreation; new life originates from the parental relationship. Otherwise, W. R. Bion's signature would remain cryptic; however, from this perspective it does make sense: Bion (1962) uses the symbols for the two sexes, male–female, as signs for the formation of new experience and, when he describes the development of thought, he speaks of conception, which implies concept formation as much as procreation. The new beginning is thus anchored in the relationship, and it must be reckoned with, as unpredictable as it is, as unlikely as it may seem, on the basis of past experiences and fixations. Precisely for this reason, the most important gift—the decisive gift that people can give each other—is the time in which the transition between farewell and new beginning can occur, and this cannot be forced.

References

Adamson, J. (1997). *Melville, Shame and the Evil Eye: A Psychoanalytic Reading*. New York: State University of New York Press.

Agamben, G. (1991). Bartleby or on contingency. In: *Potentialities* (pp. 243–271). Stanford: Stanford University Press, 1999.

Alexander, F. G., & French, T. M. (1946). *Psychoanalytic Therapy: Principles and Applications*. New York: Ronald Press.

Angehrn, E., & Küchenhoff, J. (Eds.) (2013). *Die Arbeit des Negativen. Negativität als philosophisch-psychoanalytisches Problem [The Work of the Negative: Negativity as a Philosophical-Psychoanalytical Problem]*. Weilerswist: Velbrück Wissenschaft.

Arendt, H. (1958). *The Human Condition*. Chicago: University of Chicago Press, 1998.

Arendt, H. (1978). *The Life of the Mind*. New York: Harcourt Brace Jovanovich.

Arnu, T. (2014, February 16). Stoff für Träume. *Süddeutsche Zeitung* www.sueddeutsche.de/leben/erwachsene-und-kuscheltiere-stoff-fuer-traeume-1.1888995 (last accessed 22 December 2021).

Asch, S. S. (1976). Varieties of negative therapeutic reaction and problems of technique. *Journal of the American Psychoanalytic Association, 24*(2): 383–407. https://doi.org/10.1177/000306517602400209

Augustine (397–400). *Confessions, Vol. II, Books 9–13*, C. Hammond (Ed.). Cambridge, MA: Harvard University Press (Loeb Classical Library), 2016.

Bachmann-Medick, D. (2006). The translational turn. In: D. Bachmann-Medick, *Cultural Turns: New Orientations in the Study of Culture* (pp. 175–210). Berlin: de Gruyter, 2010.

Balint, M. (1979). *The Basic Fault: Therapeutic Aspects of Regression*. London: Tavistock.

Bandia, P. (2006). African Europhone literature and writing as translation. In: T. Hermans (Ed.), *Translating Others, Vol. 2* (pp. 349–364). Brooklands: St Jerome.

Beland, H. (1999). The soft voice of the intellect: Psychoanalytic research in destructive violence and the public. *Bulletin European Psychoanalytic Federation*, 52: 6–21.

Benjamin, J. (1995). *Like Subjects, Love Objects: Essays on Recognition and Sexual Difference*. New Haven: Yale University Press.

Benjamin, W. (1921). Critique of violence. In: W. Benjamin, *Selected Writings 1, 1913–1926*, M. Bullock & M. W. Jennings (Eds.) (pp. 236–252). Cambridge, MA: Belknap Press of Harvard University Press, 1996.

Berger-Zell, C. (2013). *Abwesend und doch präsent: Wandlungen der Trauerkultur in Deutschland* [*Absent and Yet Present: Changes of the Mourning Culture in Germany*]. Neukirchen-Vluyn: Neukirchener Theologie.

Bhabha, H. K. (1994). *The Location of Culture*. London: Routledge.

Bion, W. R. (1959). Attacks on linking. *International Journal of Psycho-Analysis*, 40: 308–315.

Bion, W. R. (1962). *Learning from Experience*. London: Heinemann.

Bloch, E. (1986). *The Principle of Hope*, N. Plaice, S. Plaice, & P. Knight (Trans.). Cambridge, MA: MIT Press.

Bloom, H. (1998). *Shakespeare: The Invention of the Human*. New York: Riverhead Books.

Blumenberg, H. (1986). *Lebenszeit und Weltzeit* [*Lifetime and World Time*]. Frankfurt: Suhrkamp.

Bohleber, W. (2008). Zur Psychoanalyse der Schamerfahrungen [On the psychoanalysis of shame experiences]. *Psyche—Zeitschrift für Psychoanalyse und ihre Anwendungen*, 62: 831–839. https://doi.org/10.21706/ps-62-9-831

Böhme, H. (1997). Enthüllen und Verhüllen des Körpers in Bibel, Mythos und Kunst (mit besonderer Rücksicht auf Albrecht Dürers "Selbstbildnis als

Akt") [Uncovering and veiling the body in the Bible, myth and art, with special regard to Albrecht Dürer's "Self-Portrait as an Act"]. *Paragrana*, *6*(1): 218–247.

Boker, P. (1996). *The Grief Taboo in American Literature*. New York: New York University Press.

Bollas, C. (2013). *China on the Mind*. London: Routledge.

Borens, C. (2001). Book review: E. Vila-Matas, *Bartleby & Co. Riss*, *56*: 93–96. https://doi.org/10.1046/j.1365-2494.2001.00240.x

Brecht, B., & Bentley, E. (1965). *The Good Woman of Setzuan*. New York: Grove Press.

Britton, R. (1998). *Belief and Imagination: Explorations in Psychoanalysis*. London: Routledge.

Britton, R., & Steiner, J. (1994). Interpretation: Selected fact or overvalued idea? *International Journal of Psycho-Analysis*, *75*: 1069–1078.

Buber, M. (1970). *I and Thou*, W. Kaufmann (Trans.). New York: Scribner.

Bühler, P., & Peng-Keller, S. (Eds.) (2014). *Bildhaftes Erleben in Todesnähe. Hermeneutische Erkundungen einer heutigen ars moriendi* [*Pictorial Experience Close to Death: Hermeneutic Explorations of a Contemporary Ars Moriendi*]. Zurich: TVZ Theologischer Verlag.

Bürgin, D., & von Klitzing, K. (2001). Triadische Kompetenz: Ressource für die seelische Entwicklung [Triadic competence: Resource for mental development]. In: W. Bohleber & S. Drews (Eds.), *Die Gegenwart der Psychoanalyse—die Psychoanalyse der Gegenwart* [*The Present of Psychoanalysis: The Psychoanalysis of the Present*] (pp. 519–533). Stuttgart: Klett-Cotta.

Chase, R. (1949). *Herman Melville: A Critical Study*. New York: Macmillan.

Dahlstrom, D. (2017). Scheler on shame: A critical review. *Metodo. International Studies in Phenomenology and Philosophy*, *5*(1): 239–262. https://doi.org/10.19079/metodo.5.1.239

Deleuze, G. (1997). Bartleby or the formula. In: G. Deleuze, *Essays Critical and Clinical* (pp. 68–90), D. W. Smith & M. A. Greco (Trans.). Minneapolis: University of Minnesota Press.

Derrida, J. (1959). *Writing and Difference*. London: Routledge, 2001. https://doi.org/10.4324/9780203991787

Derrida, J. (1990). Let us not forget—psychoanalysis. *Oxford Literary Review*, *12*(1/2): 3–7. https://doi.org/10.3366/olr.1990.001

Dörr, M. (2005). *Sozialarbeit in der Psychiatrie* [*Social Work in Psychiatry*]. Munich: TTB Reinhardt.

Durst, M. (2004). Birth and natality in Hannah Arendt. In: A. T. Tymieniecka (Ed.), *Does the World Exist? Analecta Husserliana. The Yearbook of Phenomenological Research* (Volume 79). Dordrecht: Springer. https://doi.org/10.1007/978-94-010-0047-5_49

DW Akademie (2018, January 1). Asylverfahren dauern fast 11 Monate. www.dw.com/de/asylverfahren-dauern-fast-elf-monate/a-42104775 (last accessed 1 November 2021).

Erdheim, M. (1992). Das Eigene und das Fremde. Über ethnische Identität [One's own and the alien: On ethnic identity]. *Psyche: Zeitschrift für Psychoanalyse und ihre Anwendungen, 46*(8): 730–742.

Erdrich, L. (1988). *Tracks*. New York: Holt.

Feigelson, C. (1993). Personality death, object loss, and the uncanny. *International Journal of Psycho-Analysis, 74*(2): 331–345.

Fenichel, O. (1935). The scoptophilic instinct and identification. In: *The Collected Papers of Otto Fenichel, 1* (pp. 373–397). New York: Norton, 1953.

Ferenczi, S. (1988). *The Clinical Diary of Sándor Ferenczi*, J. Dupont (Ed.). Cambridge, MA: Harvard University Press.

Fink, E. (1992). Eigentod und Fremdtod [Own death and foreign death]. In: H. Ebeling (Ed.), *Der Tod in der Moderne* [*Death in the Modern Age*] (pp. 146–151). Frankfurt: Hain.

Fluck, W. (1997). *Das kulturelle Imaginäre. Funktionsgeschichte des amerikanischen Romans 1790–1900* [*The Cultural Imaginary: Functional History of the American Novel 1790–1900*]. Frankfurt: Suhrkamp.

Foucault, M. (1973). *The Birth of the Clinic: An Archaeology of Medical Perception*. New York: Vintage, 1996.

Foucault, M. (1984). *History of Sexuality, Volume 3: The Care of the Self*. New York: Vintage, 1988.

Freud, S. (1905e). Fragment of an analysis of a case of hysteria. *S. E., 7*: 7–122.

Freud, S. (1906). Letter from Sigmund Freud to Arthur Schnitzler, 8 May 1906. In: *Letters of Sigmund Freud, 1873–1979* (p. 251). London: Hogarth, 1970.

Freud, S. (1908e). Creative writers and day-dreaming. *S. E., 9*: 143–153.

Freud, S. (1910c). Leonardo da Vinci and a memory of his childhood. *S. E., 11*: 63–137.

Freud, S. (1911c). Psycho-analytic notes on an autobiographical account of a case of paranoia (Dementia paranoides). *S. E., 12*: 9–79.

Freud, S. (1912b). The dynamics of transference. *S. E., 12*: 99–108.

Freud, S. (1912e). Recommendations to physicians practising psycho-analysis. *S. E.*, *12*: 111–120.

Freud, S. (1915b). Thoughts for the times on war and death. *S. E.*, *14*: 273–300.

Freud, S. (1916d). Some character-types met with in psycho-analytic work. *S. E.*, *14*: 311–333.

Freud, S. (1917e). Mourning and melancholia. *S. E.*, *14*: 237–258.

Freud, S. (1925d). An autobiographical study. *S. E.*, *20*: 7–70.

Freud, S. (1925h). Negation. *S. E.*, *19*: 235–239.

Freud, S. (1930d). The Goethe Prize. *S. E.*, *21*: 205–214.

Gauss, K. M. (2001). A citizen in exile: The long absence of Sándor Márai. *Neue Zürcher Zeitung*, 7 April.

Green, A. (1983). *Life Narcissism, Death Narcissism*. London: Free Association, 2001.

Green, A. (1990). *Le complexe de castration*. Paris: Presses Universitaires de France.

Green, A. (1993). *The Work of the Negative*. London: Free Association, 1999.

Green, A. (2000). *Time in Psychoanalysis: Some Contradictory Aspects*. London: Free Association, 2002.

Greenson, R. (1965). The working alliance and the transference neurosis. *Psychoanalytic Quarterly*, *34*: 155–181. https://doi.org/10.1080/21674086.1965.11926343

Grinberg, L., & Grinberg, R. (1989). *Psychoanalytic Perspectives on Migration and Exile*. New Haven: Yale University Press.

Gustafsson, L. (1981). *Death of a Beekeeper*. New York: New Directions.

Han, B.-C. (1998). *Todesarten [Types of Death]*. Munich: Fink.

Han, K. (2015). *The Vegetarian*. London: Portobello.

Hansen-Löve, A., Ott, M., & Schneider, L. (Eds.) (2014). *Natalität. Geburt als Anfangsfigur in Literatur und Kunst [Natality: Birth as an Initial Figure in Literature and Art]*. Munich: Fink. https://doi.org/10.30965/9783846756386

Hassoun, J. (1995). "I would prefer not to". *Apertura*, *11*: 51–60.

Heidegger, M. (1962). *Being and Time*, J. Macquarrie & E. Robinson (Trans.). Oxford: Blackwell.

Heinrich, K. (1978). *Versuch über die Schwierigkeit Nein zu sagen [Attempt on the Difficulty of Saying No]*. Frankfurt: Stroemfeld.

Heitmeyer, W. (2010). *Deutsche Zustände [German States]*. Berlin: Suhrkamp.

Hell, D. (2003). *Soul Hunger: The Feeling Human Being and the Life Sciences*. Einsiedeln: Daimon, 2011.

Herman, J. (1997). An instance of sleep paralysis in *Moby-Dick*. *Sleep, 20*: 577–579. https://doi.org/10.1093/sleep/20.7.577

Higgins, E. T. (1987). Self-discrepancy: A theory relating self and affect. *Psychological Review, 94*(3): 319–340. https://doi.org/10.1037/0033-295X.94.3.319

Hill, N. (2016). *The Nix*. New York: Penguin Random House.

Hiscock, A., & Hopkins, L. (Eds.) (2011). *King Lear: A Critical Guide*. London: Continuum.

von Hofmannsthal, H. (1911). *Jedermann*. Munich: Deutscher Taschenbuch Verlag, 2004. *The Play of Everyman: Based on the Old English Morality Play*, G. Sterling (Trans.). Leopold Classic Library.

Holland, N. N. (1993). Psychoanalysis and literature—past and present. *Contemporary Psychoanalysis, 29*: 5–21.

Holland, N. N. (1999). Deconstruction. *International Journal of Psychoanalysis, 80*: 153–162.

Houzel, D. (2005). The trauma of birth. In: A. Mijolla (Ed.), *International Dictionary of Psychoanalysis*. Detroit: Macmillan Reference USA.

Huntington, S. P. (1996). *The Clash of Civilizations and the Remaking of World Order*. New York: Simon & Schuster.

Hynes, W. J. (1993). Mapping the characteristics of mythic tricksters: A heuristic guide. In: W. J. Hynes & W. G. Doty (Eds.), *Mythical Trickster Figures: Contours, Contexts, and Criticisms* (pp. 33–45). Tuscaloosa: University of Alabama Press.

Illich, I. (1992). Tod kontra Tod [Death versus death]. In: H. Ebeling (Ed.), *Der Tod in der Moderne* [*Death in the Modern Age*] (pp. 184–209). Frankfurt: Hain.

Iser, W. (1980). *The Act of Reading: A Theory of Aesthetic Response*. Baltimore: Johns Hopkins University Press.

Jaspers, K. (1932). *Philosophy, Vol. 2*, E. B. Ashton (Trans.). Chicago: University of Chicago Press, 1970.

Jaspers, K. (1989). The physician in the technological age. *Theoretical Medicine and Bioethics, 10*: 251–267. https://doi.org/10.1007/BF00489443

Jones, E. (1913). Review of Imago. *Zeitschrift für anwendung der psychoanalyse auf die geisteswissenschaften* [Review of the book Imago. *Zeitschrift für anwendung der psychoanalyse auf die geisteswissenschaften*, by S. Freud, O. Rank & H. Sachs]. *The Journal of Abnormal Psychology, 8*(1), 65–66. https://doi.org/10.1037/h0067441.

Jung, C. G., & Read, H. (1968). *On the Psychology of the Trickster-Figure*. London: Routledge and Kegan Paul.

Kaplan, L. (1912). Zur Psychologie des Tragischen [The psychology of tragedy]. *Imago*, 1: 132–157.

Kelly, P. (2011). The current state of thinking on *King Lear*. In: A. Hiscock & L. Hopkins (Eds.), *King Lear: A Critical Guide* (pp. 78–98). London: Continuum.

Klotz, V. (2006). *Erzählen. Von Homer zu Boccaccio, von Cervantes zu Faulkner* [*Narrating: From Homer to Boccaccio, from Cervantes to Faulkner*]. Munich: Beck.

Koch, D. (2011, November 20). Martin Luther und der Tod—sein Sermon von der Bereitung zum Sterben. https://religionheute.wordpress. com/2011/11/20/martin-luther-und-der-tod-sein-sermon-von-der-berei-tung-zum-sterben (last accessed 1 November 2021).

Koselleck, R. (1995). *Vergangene Zukunft. Zur Semantik geschichtlicher Zeiten* [*Past Future: On the Semantics of Historical Times*]. Frankfurt: Suhrkamp.

Kraus, A. (1977). *Psychose und Sozialverhalten Manisch-Depressiver* [*Psychosis and Social Behaviour of Manic-depressives*]. Stuttgart: Enke.

Kristeva, J. (1980). *Powers of Horror: An Essay on Abjection*. New York: Columbia University Press, 1982.

Kristeva, J. (1984). *Revolution in Poetic Language*. New York: Columbia University Press.

Kristeva, J. (1989). *Black Sun: Depression and Melancholia*. New York: Columbia University Press.

Kristeva, J. (1995). *New Maladies of the Soul*. New York: Columbia University Press.

Küchenhoff, J. (1998a). Körperkultur [Body culture]. In: W. Korff (Ed.), *Lexikon der Bioethik, Vol. 2* (pp. 439–443). Gütersloh: Gütersloher Verlagshaus.

Küchenhoff, J. (1998b). Trauma, Konflikt, Repräsentation [Trauma, conflict and representation]. In: A. Schlösser & K. Höhfeld (Eds.), *Trauma und Konflikt* [*Trauma and Conflict*] (pp. 13–33). Gießen: Psychosozial-Verlag.

Küchenhoff, J. (2012). *Körper und Sprache. Theoretische und klinische Beiträge zu einem intersubjektiven Verständnis des Körpererlebens* [*Body and Language: Theoretical and Clinical Contributions to an Intersubjective Understanding of Body Experience*]. Gießen: Psychosozial-Verlag.

Küchenhoff, J. (2013). *Der Sinn im Nein und die Gabe des Gesprächs. Psychoanalytisches Verstehen zwischen Philosophie und Klinik* [*The Sense in the No and the Gift of Dialogue: Psychoanalytical Understanding between Philosophy and Clinic*]. Weilerswist: Velbrück Wissenschaft.

Küchenhoff, J. (2018). *Understanding Psychosis: A Psychoanalytic Approach*. London: Routledge. https://doi.org/10.4324/9781351025942

Küchenhoff, J., & Agarwalla, P. (2012). *Körperbild und Persönlichkeit* [*Body Image and Personality*]. Heidelberg: Springer. https://doi.org/10.1007/978-3-642-22472-0

Küchenhoff, J., & Warsitz, R. P. (2012). *Labyrinthe des Ohres. Vom therapeutischen Sinn des Zuhörens in Psychopathologie und Psychoanalyse* [*Labyrinths of the Ear: On the Therapeutic Meaning of Listening in Psychopathology and Psychoanalysis*]. Würzburg: Königshausen & Neumann.

Kürzere Asylverfahren reduzieren Arbeitslosigkeit [Shorter asylum proceedings reduce unemployment] (2016, August 4). *SRF Schweizer Radio und Fernsehen*. www.srf.ch/news/schweiz/kuerzere-asylverfahren-reduzieren-arbeitslosigkeit (last accessed 1 November 2021).

Lacan, J. (1945). Logical time and the assertion of anticipated certainty. In: J. Lacan, *Écrits: The First Complete Edition in English*, B. Fink (Trans.) (pp. 161–175). New York: Norton, 2006.

Lacan, J. (1949). The mirror stage as formative of the I function as revealed in psychoanalytic experience. In: J. Lacan, *Écrits: The First Complete Edition in English*, B. Fink (Trans.) (pp. 75–81). New York: Norton, 2006.

Lacan, J. (1953). The function and field of speech and language in psychoanalysis. In: J. Lacan, *Écrits: The First Complete Edition in English*, B. Fink (Trans.) (pp. 197–268). New York: Norton, 2006.

Lacan, J. (1958). On a question prior to any possible treatment of psychosis. In: J. Lacan, *Écrits: The First Complete Edition in English*, B. Fink (Trans.) (pp. 445–488). New York: Norton, 2006.

Lacan, J. (2006). *Écrits: The First Complete Edition in English*, B. Fink (Trans.). New York: Norton.

Lambert, M. (Ed.) (2004). *Handbook of Psychotherapy and Behavior Change* (5th edn). London: Wiley.

Lang, H. (1980). Struktural-analytische Aspekte der Subjektivität [Structural-analytical aspects of subjectivity]. In: F. Kittler (Ed.), *Austreibung des Geistes aus den Geisteswissenschaften* [*Expulsion of the Mind from the Humanities*] (pp. 188–203). Paderborn: Schöningh.

Laplanche, J. (1988). *Die allgemeine Verführungstheorie und andere Aufsätze* [*The General Theory of Seduction*]. Tübingen: Edition Diskord.

Laqueur, T. (2015). *The Work of the Dead: A Cultural History of Mortal Remains*. New Jersey: Princeton University Press. https://doi.org/10.2307/j.ctvc77h3r

Lear, J. (2006). *Radical Hope: Ethics in the Face of Cultural Devastation.* Cambridge, MA: Harvard University Press.

von Lersner, U., & Kizilhan, J. I. (2017). *Kultursensitive Psychotherapie* [*Culture-sensitive Psychotherapy*]. Göttingen: Hogrefe. https://doi.org/10.1026/02755-000

Levinas, E. (1984). *Die Zeit und der Andere* [*Time and the Other*]. Hamburg: Meiner.

Levy, S. T., & Inderbitzin, L. B. (1989). Negativism and countertransference. *Journal of the American Psychoanalytic Association, 37*(1): 377–430. https://doi.org/10.1177/000306518903700102

Loch, W. (1993). *The Art of Interpretation: Deconstruction and New Beginning in the Psychoanalytic Process.* London: Routledge, 2006.

Lorenzer, A. (2006). *Szenisches Verstehen. Zur Erkenntnis des Unbewussten* [*Scenic Understanding: On the Knowledge of the Unconscious*]. Marburg: Tectum.

Lütkehaus, L. (1999). *Nichts* [*Nothing*]. Zurich: Haffmans.

Machleidt, W., & Gün, A. K. (2011). Tiefenpsychologische Behandlung interkulturell [Intercultural depth psychology treatment]. In: W. Machleidt & A. Heinz (Eds.), *Praxis der interkulturellen Psychiatrie und Psychotherapie* [*Practice of Intercultural Psychiatry and Psychotherapy*] (pp. 401–413). Munich: Urban & Fischer. https://doi.org/10.1016/B978-3-437-24570-1.10039-X

Mahler, M., Pine, F., & Bergman, A. (1975). *Psychological Birth of the Human Infant.* New York: Basic Books.

Márai, S. (1942). *Embers,* C. B. Janeway (Trans.). New York: Random House, 2002.

Marcus Aurelius (170–180). *Meditations, with Selected Correspondence,* R. Hard & C. Gill (Eds.). Oxford: Oxford University Press, 2011.

Marquard, O. (2013). *Endlichkeitsphilosophisches. Über das Altern* [*Philosophy of Finiteness: About Ageing*]. Stuttgart: Reclam.

von Matt, P. (1995). *Verkommene Söhne, missratene Töchter. Familiendesaster in der Literatur* [*Deteriorated Sons, Ill-bred Daughters: Family Disasters in Literature*]. Munich: Hanser.

McDougall, J. (1989). *Theatres of the Body: A Psychoanalytic Approach to Psychosomatic Illness.* London: Free Association.

McDougall, J. (2013). *Theatres of the Mind: Illusion and Truth on the Psychoanalytic Stage.* New York: Routledge. https://doi.org/10.4324/9780203727393

Melville, H. (1985). Bartleby the Scrivener. In: H. Melville, *Billy Budd, Sailor, and Other Stories* (pp. 57–100). London: Penguin.

Melville, H. (2001). *Moby-Dick.* www.gutenberg.org/files/2701/2701-h/2701-h. htm (last accessed 1 November 2021).

Menninghaus, W. (1999). *Ekel. Theorie und Geschichte einer starken Empfindung* [*Disgust: The Theory and History of a Strong Sensation*]. Frankfurt: Suhrkamp.

Menninghaus, W. (2003). *Disgust: The Theory and History of a Strong Sensation.* New York: State University of New York Press.

Merleau-Ponty, M. (1962). *Phenomenology of Perception.* London: Routledge.

Merleau-Ponty, M. (1965). *Signs* (9th edn). Evanston, IL: Northwestern University Press.

Miller, E. H. (1975). *Melville.* New York: Braziller.

MLA International Bibliography. www.mla.org/Publications/MLA-International-Bibliography (last accessed 1 November 2021).

Money-Kyrle, R. (1978). *The Collected Papers of Roger Money-Kyrle*, D. Meltzer (Ed.). Strath Tay: Clunie.

Ogden, T. (1994). The analytic third: Working with intersubjective clinical facts. *International Journal of Psycho-Analysis, 75*(1): 3–19.

OPD Task Force (2009). *Operationalized Psychodynamic Diagnostics OPD-2* (2nd rev. edn). Bern: Huber.

Özbek, T. (2006). Autonomieentwicklung und Identität im transkulturellen Alltag [Autonomy development and identity in transcultural everyday life]. In: E. Wohlfart & M. Zaumseil (Eds.), *Transkulturelle Psychiatrie—interkulturelle Psychotherapie* [*Transcultural Psychiatry: Intercultural Psychotherapy*] (pp. 95–110). Berlin: Springer. https://doi.org/10.1007/978-3-540-32776-9_6

Özbek, T., & Wohlfart, E. (2006). Der transkulturelle Übergangsraum [The transcultural transitional space]. In: E. Wohlfart, & M. Zaumseil (Eds.), *Transkulturelle Psychiatrie—interkulturelle Psychotherapie* [*Transcultural Psychiatry: Intercultural Psychotherapy*] (pp. 169–176). Berlin: Springer. https://doi.org/10.1007/978-3-540-32776-9_11

Peniazek, Z. (1982). The experience of time and hope in the elderly. *Contemporary Psychoanalysis, 18*(4): 635–645. https://doi.org/10.1080/00107530.1982.10745708

Putnam, R. B. (2000). *Bowling Alone: The Collapse and Revival of American Community.* New York: Simon & Schuster. https://doi.org/10.1145/358916.361990

Radin, P., Kerényi, K., & Jung, C. G. (1954). *Der göttliche Schelm. Ein indianischer Mythen-Zyklus* [*The Divine Prankster: An Indian Myth Cycle*]. Zurich: Rhein-Verlag.

Rank, O. (1914). Der Doppelgänger. Eine psychoanalytische Studie. In: *Imago*, 3: 97–164.

Rank, O. (1929). *The Trauma of Birth*. Chelmsford: Courier Corporation.

Rank, O. (1971). *The Double: A Psychoanalytic Study*, Harry Tucker (Trans.). Chapel Hill: The University of North Carolina Press.

Richter, H. E. (1962). *Eltern, Kind und Neurose* [*Parents, Child and Neurosis*]. Reinbek: Rowohlt.

Ricœur, P. (1998). *Das Rätsel der Vergangenheit. Erinnern—Vergessen— Verzeihen* [*The Mystery of the Past: Remembering—Forgetting— Forgiveness*]. Göttingen: Wallstein.

Roth, P. (1994). *Portnoy's Complaint*. New York: Random House.

Roth, P. (2001). *The Human Stain*. New York: Random House.

Roth, P. (2005). *Everyman*. New York: Random House.

Roth, P. (2008). *Indignation*. Boston: Houghton Mifflin.

Roth, P. (2009). *The Humbling*. Boston: Houghton Mifflin.

Roth, P. (2010). *Nemesis*. New York: Random House.

Sachs, H. (1913). Die Motivgestaltung bei Schnitzler [Motive formation by Schnitzler]. *Imago*, 2: 302–318.

Sadger, I. (1912). Von der Pathographie zur Psychographie [From pathography to psychography]. *Imago*, 1: 158–175.

Schafer, R. (2000). Reflections on "thinking in the presence of others". *International Journal of Psycho-Analysis*, 81: 85–96.

Schahadat, S. (2013). Übersetzen: Text—Kultur—"translational turn" [Translate: Text—culture—translational turn]. In: C. Dathe, R. Makarska, & S. Shahadat (Eds.), *Zwischentexte. Literarisches Übersetzen in Theorie und Praxis* [*Intermediate Texts: Literary Translation in Theory and Practice*] (pp. 19–46). Berlin: Frank & Timme.

Scheffler, S. (2013). *Death and the Afterlife*. Oxford: Oxford University Press. https://doi.org/10.1093/acprof:oso/9780199982509.001.0001

Scheler, M. (1987). Shame and feelings of modesty. In: M. Scheler, *Person and Self-Value: Three Essays*, Ed. M. S. Frings (pp. 1–85). Dordrecht: Nijhoff. https://doi.org/10.1007/978-94-009-3503-7

Sen, A. (2006). *Identity and Violence: The Illusion of Destiny—Issues of Our Time*. New York: Norton.

Shakespeare, W. (2000). *The History of King Lear*, S. Wells (Ed.), on the basis of a text prepared by G. Taylor (The Oxford Shakespeare). Oxford: Clarendon Press.

Simpson, D. (1982). *Fetishism and Imagination: Dickens, Melville, Conrad*. Baltimore: Johns Hopkins University Press.

Stern, D. N. (1985). *The Interpersonal World of the Infant*. London: Routledge.

Stern, D. N., Sander, L. W., Nahum, J. P., Harrison, A. M., Lyons-Ruth, K., Morgan, A. C., Bruschweiler-Stern, N., & Tronick, E. Z. (1998). Non-interpretive mechanisms in psychoanalytic therapy: The "something more" than interpretation. *International Journal of Psycho-Analysis*, 79(5): 903–921.

Sternberger, D. (1981). *Über den Tod* [*On Death*]. Frankfurt: Suhrkamp.

Straub, J. (2002). *Transitorische Identität* [*Transitional Identity*]. Frankfurt: Campus.

Süddeutsche Zeitung (2014, February 16). www.sueddeutsche.de/leben/erwachsene-und-kuscheltiere-stoff-fuer-traeume-1.1888995 (last accessed 30 December 2021).

Taylor, C. (2007). *A Secular Age*. Cambridge, MA: Belknap Press of Harvard University Press. https://doi.org/10.2307-/j.ctvxrpz54

Tenenbaum, D. (2006). Race, class, and shame in the fiction of Philip Roth. *Shofar: An Interdisciplinary Journal of Jewish Studies*, 24(4): 34–49. https://doi.org/10.1353/sho.2006.0110

Terkessidis, M. (2010). *Interkultur* [*Interculture*]. Berlin: Suhrkamp.

Theunissen, M. (1965). *The Other: Studies in the Social Ontology of Husserl, Heidegger, Sartre, and Buber*. Cambridge, MA: MIT Press, 1984.

Thomä, H. (1984). Der "Neubeginn" Michael Balints (1932) aus heutiger Sicht [Michael Balint's "recommencement" (1932) in retrospective]. *Psyche—Zeitschrift für Psychoanalyse und ihre Anwendungen*, 38(6): 516–543.

Thompson, L. (1952). *Melville's Quarrel with God*. Princeton: Princeton University Press. https://doi.org/10.1515/9781400878161

Todorov, T. (1995). *Memory as a Remedy*. London: Seagull, 2010.

Tolchin, M. (1988). *Mourning, Gender and Creativity in the Art of Herman Melville*. New Haven: Yale University Press. https://doi.org/10.2307/1908685

Trump, D. (2020, August 20). www.presidency.ucsb.edu/documents/remarks-briefing-border-wall-construction-yuma-arizona (last accessed 21 November 2021).

Tugendhat, E. (2006). *Über den Tod* [*On Death*]. Frankfurt: Suhrkamp.

Vila-Matas, E. (2001). *Bartleby & Co.* New York: New Directions, 2007.

Wagner, B. (2012). Kulturelle Übersetzung. Erkundungen über ein wanderndes Konzept [Cultural translation: Explorations of a wandering concept]. In: A. Babka, J. Malle, & M. Schmidt (Eds.), *Dritte Räume. Homi K. Bhabhas Kulturtheorie. Anwendung, Kritik, Reflexion* [*Third Rooms: Homi Bhabha's Cultural Theory—Application, Criticism, Reflection*] (pp. 29–42). Wien: Turia + Kant.

Walsh, D. (2010). The birth and death of a diagnosis: Monomania in France, Britain and in Ireland. *Irish Journal of Psychological Medicine, 31*: 39–45. https://doi.org/10.1017/ipm.2013.65

Watzlawick, P., Beavin, J. H., & Jackson, D. D. (1967). *Pragmatics of Human Communication: A Study of Interactional Patterns, Pathologies and Paradoxes.* New York: Norton.

Weaver, R. (1921). *Herman Melville: Mariner and Mystic.* New York: Doran.

Wells, S. (2000). Introduction. In: W. Shakespeare, *The History of King Lear*, S. Wells (Ed.), on the basis of a text prepared by G. Taylor (pp. 1–80). Oxford: Clarendon Press.

Wikipedia (2021, August 23). https://de.wikipedia.org/wiki/Erstaufnahmeeinrichtung_(Deutschland) (last accessed 1 November 2021).

Wikipedia (2021, October 21). https://en.wikipedia.org/wiki/The_miller,_his_son_and_the_donkey (last accessed 1 November 2021).

Winnicott, D. W. (1953). Transitional objects and transitional phenomena: A study of the first not-me possession. *International Journal of Psycho-Analysis, 34*(2): 89–97.

Winnicott, D. W. (1969). The use of an object. *International Journal of Psycho-Analysis, 50*(11): 712–716.

Wurmser, L. (1981). *The Mask of Shame.* Baltimore: Johns Hopkins University Press.

Wyss, D. (1973). *Beziehung und Gestalt* [*Relationship and Gestalt*]. Göttingen: Vandenhoeck & Ruprecht.

Zeltner, E. (2001). *Sándor Márai. Ein Leben in Bildern* [*Sándor Márai: A Life in Pictures*]. Munich: Piper.

Index